Daily Meditations (with Scripture)

for Busy Dads

Patrick T. Reardon

ACTA Publications

Chicago, Illinois

For Cathy,

and David and Sarah

Daily Meditations (with Scripture) for Busy Dads
by Patrick T. Reardon

Edited by Gregory F. Augustine Pierce
Cover Artwork by Isz
Design and Typesetting by Garrison Publications

Special thanks to Helen Reichert Lambin and Suzette
Arsipe Lambin for help in choosing the Scripture
passages.

Scripture quotations are from the *New Revised
Standard Version* of the Bible, copyright 1989 by the
Division of Christian Education of the National
Council of the Churches of Christ in the USA. All
rights reserved. Used by permission.

Library of Congress Catalog number: 95–78804

ISBN: 0-87946-128-4

Printed in the United States of America

99 98 97   5 4 3

New Year's Day

The children rise early and crawl into bed with us. They cuddle and chatter. They talk of taking the sled out in the snow. Their noses run with mid-winter colds.

They eat breakfast, get dressed, set up their toys near the Christmas tree and play their games.

My five-year-old daughter sees a bird land on the ledge outside the window. She can hardly contain her delight.

My eight-year-old son doesn't notice. He's drawing a picture of a basketball player. A look of concentration fills his face.

It's just another day. Just another year. Just another beginning.

God saw everything that he had made, and indeed, it was very good. Genesis 1:31

Ah, Fatherhood

Your son walks by your chair, aimlessly.

You reach out and pull him up on your lap.

He leans back into your shoulder.

You rest your cheek on his head. The short hair of his buzz haircut make a pleasant prickly feeling against your skin.

Ah, fatherhood.

Then little children were being brought to him in order that he might lay his hands on them and pray. Matthew 19:13

Shoveling

I go out to shovel the snow. I like the work. It's good exercise, and the falling snow is beautiful to watch. I start on the front walk.

After a while, I look up and see that the walk along the side of the house is already shoveled.

At the end of the walk, my eight-year-old son is playing in the snow. I call to him: "Did you shovel the walk?"

"Yes," he shouts back, and he raises his arms like a muscle-man.

It is a turning point. It is the first time he has done real, helpful work by himself.

He goes back to playing in the snow.

When I was a child I spoke like a child, I thought like a child, I reasoned like a child; when I became an adult, I put an end to childish ways. 1 Corinthians 13:11.

| City |

He likes living in the city. He likes it that his children are growing up in the middle of a place of such life and diversity.

He likes the mix of people that his children see and meet and make friends with.

He likes the wealth of experiences they have—from walking to the corner store to riding the subway, from visiting a museum on their own to eating at an Iranian restaurant.

But living in the city also means living amid the crime and drugs and gangs.

He doesn't like that part of living in the city. And he worries.

For here we have no lasting city, but we are looking for the city that is to come. Hebrews 13:14

Home Alone

Your first-grade daughter's home from school. She's got a bad cold, but she's enjoying herself and her day of freedom. She's playing with her dolls.

It's time to drive to school to pick up your son, but the idea of getting your daughter dressed and taking her out in the cold seems like too much of a hassle.

Besides, she pleads, "Oh, Dad, I can stay by myself."

So you decide: Okay. You'll leave her alone for the ten minutes it takes to get to the school and back. You'll leave her alone in the house for the first time in her life—and yours.

You're back right away. But something's changed.

Your little daughter's not so little anymore. She's taken another step on the road to her own life. She's taken another step—and you've helped her—on the road to leaving your home.

It is a bittersweet moment.

———————————

Solid food is for the mature, for those whose facilities have been trained by practice to distinguish good from evil. Hebrews 5:14

Jump

His daughter is dressed in a spur-of-the-moment costume. A blanket is a hood and cape. Sunglasses add to the mystery.

She stands there, next to his chair, waiting to be noticed.

But his wife is talking to him about the mortgage, and about a $365 repair to the furnace, and about a way-too-expensive outing she wants the family to take.

With each new item, his aggravation level rises another notch. And, when he finally notices his daughter standing there, waiting to be discovered, he growls, "Get back. You're crowding me too much."

She jumps, startled. Her body, her face, register her surprise.

He hates it that he makes her jump like that.

Unjust anger cannot be justified, /for anger tips the scale to one's ruin. /Those who are patient stay calm until the right moment, /and then cheerfulness comes back to them. Sirach 1:22-23

When Work Is Good

Work is going apace. I'm in a rhythm. Things are fitting into place. There are moderate bursts of activity, balanced by breathing spaces. There are solid triumphs, no major failures.

It can't last.

For we are what he has made us, created in Christ Jesus for good works, which God prepared beforehand to be our way of life.
Ephesians 2:10

> *How?*

How can he discipline his daughter when she sasses him? That's exactly what he wanted to do to his old man—but never did—when he was her age.

How can he say no to his son's demand for expensive toys? That's exactly what he yearned for—but never got—when he was his age.

How can he refuse to drive his children here and there, to play board games with them, to listen to their long, rambling, unfocused stories?

That's what he always wanted his father to do.

———————————————

Do nothing without deliberation, /but when you have acted, do not regret it. /Do not go on a path full of hazards, /and do not stumble at an obstacle twice. Sirach 32:19-20

The Weight

He leaves the hospital and heads for home. The long-familiar apartment is empty now, but, in a few short days, it will be filled with new life.

He leaves his wife and their new son up on the fourth floor of the hospital. She is asleep, and so is the baby. He leaves his new family and heads for home.

He is alone, heading home for sleep after the long delivery. He is alone, but, of course, he isn't.

He carries a new weight on his shoulders—the responsibility for nurturing, preserving and guiding this new life.

He is a father now.

For the moment, it is an awkward burden. He is unsure of himself, and more than a little afraid.

For you have been my help, /and in the shadow of your wings I sing for joy. Psalm 63:7

January 10

John Wayne

My son thinks it's too bad that I don't cry. He knows it feels good, emptying, freeing. He knows his mom cries easily. He's not ashamed of tears. It's a mystery to him that I am.

What's wrong with tears? Nothing.

But John Wayne never cried. So, neither do I.

Jesus began to weep. John 11:35

Competition

Your son has been competing with you. For a long time, you didn't even notice.

You thought he was just being loud. You were distracted by his antics, irritated.

He was interrupting you. He was pushing his sister around. He was swearing. He was talking back.

He crowed too loud when he answered the TV sports quiz before you.

No wonder you were irritated.

Your son is growing up.

Again I saw that under the sun the race is not to the swift, nor the battle to the strong, nor bread to the wise, nor riches to the intelligent, nor favor to the skillful; but time and chance happen to them all. Ecclesiastes 9:11

> *Grandfather*

Your son is now a father.

You see him change his own baby's diaper. She's a girl. And you remember—no, really, you can't remember—what it was like to change your son's diapers.

Was he ever really a baby you held in your arms? Did he ever burp up, like his daughter does now, with such vehemence?

Well, yes. But what you remember is this: that day on vacation when, suddenly, he walked three steps across the room.

To you.

Grandchildren are the crown of the aged, /and the glory of children is their parents. Proverbs 17:6

The Meaning of Fatherhood: Part 1

Fatherhood means going to a single friend's apartment and picturing how your children would take his huge collection of CDs—how can he afford so many?—and fling them Frisbee-like around the room.

It's noticing the absence of fingerprints on his walls.

It's seeing his glass coffee table, unbroken and unprotected.

It's remembering a time when tidiness was a possibility, when everything had its place and stayed there, when chauffeuring wasn't part of your job description.

But your single friend doesn't have Halloween drawings decorating his desk at work. And he doesn't know the arms-legs-total-body hug of a tired child ready for bed.

Your children will be like olive shoots /around your table. /Thus shall the man be blessed /who fears the LORD. Psalm 128:3-4

$$\boxed{\textit{Stories}}$$

It's bedtime, and I'm home alone with the kids. This is my wife's late night at the office.

It's been a busy day at work. I'm drained. I can hardly wait for the children to fall asleep so I can sit in the quiet of the darkened apartment under a reading lamp and, well, nod off to sleep.

But the kids want their bedtime stories. My five-year-old wants me to read her a book about Cinderella. Then my eight-year-old wants me to tell him a story—"something about you when you were a little kid."

I love how they enjoy stories. I think it is a great gift that my wife and I have given them, something that will enrich their entire lives.

But, tonight, I'm soooo tired.

Each of you must give as you have made up your mind, not reluctantly or under compulsion, for God loves a cheerful giver.
2 Corinthians 9:7

Unknown

They talked about it not a few times—on birthdays, at anniversaries, during moments of particular intimacy. They talked about it seriously, but always with a touch of humor. It was as if they were playing.

He would die first. That's what the actuarial tables showed. She would live on. All their plans were based on this.

And now it's here.

It's earlier than expected. It's so very much more painful than they could have imagined.

They are in some deep sea together. And this is where they will separate.

He will go, still too young. She will stay.

She will stay with the bills and the children and the sunrises and the lost keys. She will grieve.

He will dive into the unknown.

———————————

Listen, I will tell you a mystery! We will not all die, but we will all be changed, in a moment, in the twinkling of an eye, at the last trumpet. For the trumpet will sound and the dead will be raised imperishable, and we will be changed. 1 Corinthians 15:51-52

> ## *Morning Song*

Let's go. Come on. Let's go.

Let's go. Come on. Let's go.

Put your clothes on.

Eat your breakfast.

Brush your teeth.

Get in the car.

Let's go. Come on. Let's go.

Let's go. Come on. Let's go.

Close the door.

Buckle your seat belt.

Stop fighting.

Put your hat back on.

Let's go. Come on. Let's go.

Let's go. Come on. Let's go.

---

*The mighty one, God the LORD, /speaks and
summons the earth /from the rising of the sun to
its setting. Psalm 50:1*

Voicemail I

"Hi, Dad. This is your daughter.

"I'm just calling to say I love you. And that's it.

"Bye-bye . . . . bye-bye."

On that day I will answer, says the Lord, /I will answer the heavens /and they shall answer the earth. Hosea 2:21

A Sunny, Cold Afternoon

Our daughter is spending the afternoon at a friend's house, so my wife and I are going to do something special with our eight-year-old son—just the three of us, a rare treat.

Over lunch, we weigh our options. Since it is so very cold this day, we decide to stay home and watch a video together, all warm and cozy.

But, when I pop in the cassette, the machine won't work. I try this and that, but it's broken. Nothing I can do can get it to work. And I'm frustrated.

The hell with it. I go take a nap.

When I awake, my excited son tells me how he and his mom spent the whole afternoon sewing, knitting and crocheting.

"I'm so glad the video didn't work," he says.

The human mind may devise many plans, but it is the purpose of the Lord that will be established. Proverbs 19:21

Divorce

Sometimes the kids side with him. Sometimes with their mother.

They're worn out from picking sides.

He's worn out, too.

So is his wife.

_____

Better is a dry morsel with quiet /then a house full of feasting with strife. Proverbs 17:1

> ### *Missing the Point*

He says: "My father was brilliant, wonderfully educated, erudite, witty, clever, widely respected and nationally recognized as an expert in his field."

He says: "My father always wanted to argue and debate. You knew as soon as you met him that he was a lawyer."

He says: "My father loved to compete. He bought two small machines one Christmas and raced me to see which of us could put one together first. He won."

Fathers, do not provoke your children, or they may lose heart. Colossians 3:21

Mystery

I miss the mystery church had when I was growing up. I miss the formality of the ritual, the priest in his stiff, colorful vestments. I miss the Latin; somehow, it seemed like a secret code to God.

I miss the tall candles, and the bells that the altar boys would ring when the host was lifted. (At our church, we had a mini-keyboard that rang chimes at the consecration.)

Mass now is in the school gym. I like that, too. I like our dialogue homily, and I like how, after the service, we stick around and talk to each other over coffee and rolls. I like how the kids play in the same space where we worship.

This new way is a better way. But, in a deep corner of my heart, I miss the art and beauty of that earlier way.

Without any doubt, the mystery of our religion is great: He was revealed in flesh, /vindicated in spirit, /seen by angels, /proclaimed among Gentiles, /believed in throughout the world, /taken up in glory. 1 Timothy 3:16

Money

Don't talk to him about money. He doesn't want to hear it. He doesn't want to talk about it. He wants to pretend there's nothing wrong.

He has to face the mortgage, and the car payments, and the tuition, and the insurance bills, and the repair bills, and the VISA bill.

He feels squeezed by his need for money. The thought of money makes him tense.

He feels cornered.

"So do not worry about tomorrow, for tomorrow wll bring worries of its own. Today's trouble is enough for today."
Matthew 6:34

Dancing

My children are both good dancers, though in different ways.

My eight-year-old son can do the hard, jerky, sharp, syncopated movements of rap and rock music.

My five-year-old daughter dances to the same music in a more flowing fashion, a style more akin to Isadora Duncan than Janet Jackson.

I never learned to dance. I just lumber across the dance floor. I wish I could learn now, but it's too late.

Unless, maybe, they could teach me.

David danced before the LORD with all his might. 2 Samuel 6:14

Stupid Boss Tricks

Are all bosses stupid?

Or just mine?

This new assignment is pointless, onerous and impossible to carry out the way he wants it carried out.

It came from the top boss who gave it to the middle boss who gave it to my boss who gave it to me. I have no one I can pawn it off on.

I'll have to carry it out the best I can. I'll have to find some way to make it useful, rewarding and do-able.

Must I?

Yes, I must.

Then the Israelite supervisors came to Pharaoh and cried, "Why do you treat your servants like this? No straw is given to your servants, yet they say to us, 'Make bricks!' Look how your servants are beaten! You are unjust to your own people." Exodus 5:15-16

Occupation: Father

Imagine this:

At a cocktail party in a high-rise apartment building in Manhattan, the well-dressed guests mingle, sipping drinks and daintily tasting hors d'oeuvres.

The room is filled with the music of a string quartet and the hum of energetic conversation.

Two men nod to each other and introduce themselves.

"What do you do?" one asks.

The other responds without missing a beat: "I'm a father."

"Here am I and the children whom God has given me." Hebrews 2:13

Busy

You're too busy for household chores. Your wife takes care of those, even though she works, too.

She calls the babysitter. She schedules the repair people. She buys the kids' clothes. She gets the car washed. She fixes the kids' lunches. She does the laundry. She bakes the cookies for the school sale.

Sometimes, you feel guilty.

But then you get busy again.

"For what will it profit them to gain the whole world and forfeit their life?" Mark 8:36

My Super Son

My son says: "I'm the greatest basketball player in the world. I'm as good as Michael Jordon. No, I'm better."

My son says: "I like to draw. I draw real good. I draw better than Michelangelo and Raphael put together."

I say: "Go for it!"

_____

Even youths will faint and be weary, /and the young will fall exhausted; /but those who wait for the LORD shall renew their strength. /they shall mount up with wings like eagles, /they shall run and not be weary, /they shall walk and not faint. Isaiah 40:31

What's Worse

It's bad enough when you've told your kids what to do to succeed, and then they don't do it and get in trouble.

What's worse is when they run into problems and you didn't warn them and don't know what to say to them afterward.

All this I have tested by wisdom; I said, "I will be wise," but it was far from me. Ecclesiastes 7:23

Nanay

The other woman—the one who had promised she would take care of our son when my wife returned to work, the one who played classical music in her home and promised a day full of "enriching" activities for the children in her care—had said no at the last minute. Even though everything had been arranged, she backed out on us.

We were desperate. The busybody of our neighborhood steered us to a Filipino grandmother a half block away. We went to talk to her.

She was shy about her heavily accented English. Her townhouse was small and crowded with her adult children and the other small children she watched as well. The TV was on too much. She didn't play classical music to the kids.

But we were in a bind, and she seemed to be a warm person. So we left our son with her—at least until we could find a better place.

Eight years later, he's a third-grader, but he still goes to her house after school. And so does his sister. They call her Nanay. That's the word for "mother" in Tagalog, the language of the Philippines.

In our family, it's also another word for love.

Beloved, let us love one another, because love is from God; everyone who loves is born of God and knows God. 1 John 4:7

> *Instant Agenda*

I have the day off. She has the day off.

We loll together in bed, talking and playing. The morning sun comes in the window. We recall old jokes from our dating days. Our talk has no direction. It lacks purpose. It has no agenda. We are relaxed.

Then, the kids come in, asking for breakfast.

Instant agenda.

Jesus said to them, "Come and have break-fast." Now none of the disciples dared to ask him, "Who are you?" because they knew it was the Lord. John 21:12

The Trial

He sits in the courtroom and watches his twenty-eight-year-old daughter stand trial for trespassing at a U.S. Navy installation built to communicate with nuclear submarines.

His daughter tries to say that she was there to protest the immorality of nuclear weapons. But the judge cuts her off.

She tries to say it's okay to break the law by climbing over the fence at the installation and singing peace songs to the workers because there's a higher moral law that governs in this case. But the judge cuts her off.

Her father would scream out if his life had been such that he had learned how to scream out. Instead, he holds his feelings inside—his fear that his daughter will have to go to jail and his pride that his little girl is standing up to the entire government and his anger that she isn't getting her chance to talk.

Convicted, his daughter refuses to pay the fine and declares she will accept time in jail. But the judge cuts her off. "There are people in this country," the judge says, "who belong in jail. You are not one of them. I'm going to revoke your driving privileges for five years. This case is closed."

Silently, the father walks to his daughter and hugs her. He has too many words to say to be able to say anything.

The word of God is not chained. 2 Timothy 2:9

Angry

I'm embarrassed when I get angry and slam doors and shout. Usually, it has nothing to do with anything my wife or kids have done. It's a built-up tension for which I haven't found a better release. It's childish. And there you have it.

The kids are young, but already they know enough to talk back to me and tell me when I'm overdoing it.

That's better than having them be afraid or feel it's their fault, of course. But it's too much responsibility for them to have to carry.

One who is slow to anger is better than the mighty, /and one whose temper is controlled than one who captures a city. Proverbs 16:32

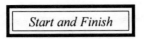

Start and Finish

She's carrying your child in her body. You have an odd thought.

It really isn't your child. Or hers.

The life you and she have sparked is another person, independent and free.

This person, after taking that first journey from the dark, warm inner sea to the light, air and cold, will grow.

This person will stretch.

This person will choose.

What you and she have started, this person will finish.

See, the former things have come to pass, /and new things I now declare; /before they spring forth, /I tell you of them. Isaiah 42:9

Awake

With the mother at work, the father wakes the children, gets them dressed and feeds them.

It's never so simple.

There's the jolly cajoling. ("Up and at 'em! Rise and shine!")

When that doesn't work, there's the peremptory order. ("Okay, enough of this, get up now!")

Finally, there's the hard bargaining. ("All right, if you get dressed now, I'll let you lay down again for five minutes.")

And he hasn't even started to think about breakfast yet.

Sleeper, awake! /Rise from the dead, /and Christ will shine on you. Ephesians 5:14

Odd Noise

Something is wrong. He's not sure what's the matter, but he's certain that something is.

He looks over at his wife. She's still asleep. The sun is already up on this winter morning. And he raises his head to listen and look.

Did he hear a sound? No, that wasn't what woke him.

Was there some movement outside the bedroom door? No, he doesn't think so. Everything's quiet now. All is still.

He grows more worried the longer he can't figure out what is wrong. He starts to lift the blanket off and slide his legs out of bed.

"Are you getting up, honey?" his sleepy wife asks. "I thought for sure you'd sleep in since the kids are at my mother's."

He slides back under the covers and luxuriates in the odd noise of silence.

Now there was a great wind, so strong that it was splitting mountains and breaking rocks in pieces before the LORD, but the LORD was not in the wind; and after the wind an earthquake, but the LORD was not in the earthquake; and after the earthquake a fire, but the LORD was not in the fire; and after the fire a sound of sheer silence. When Elijah heard it, he wrapped his face in his mantle and went out and stood at the entrance of the cave. 1 Kings 19:11-13

Four Love Stories

One says: "My father patted me on the back."

A second says: "My father played catch with me."

A third says: "My father stayed home from work to care for me when I was ill."

A fourth says: "My father hugged me every time he saw me."

"You are the light of the world. . . . Let your light shine before others, so that they may see your good works and give glory to your Father in heaven." Matthew 5:14,16

Assertive

You're a fairly quiet, even shy, guy. You don't like to bring attention to yourself. You never make a scene. You keep things to yourself.

But in the supermarket, when your five-year-old daughter says, "Dad, I've got to go to the bathroom bad," you set aside your insecurities and find a stockboy and get directions to the bathroom in the storeroom.

It's easy to be assertive when your teacher is a five-year-old in danger of wetting her pants.

Let the wise also hear and gain in learning,
/and the discerning acquire skill. Proverbs 1:5

Sick at Church

My son gets sick at church. Not really ill in the throwing-up-all-over-the-place sense, but his stomach is queasy and his head is spinning.

So I take him home before the end of the service. My wife and daughter stay behind.

I want to give him medicine, but he says, "No, it tastes bad." So I lead him to bed and tell him to lay down for awhile. I put a bucket next to the bed in case he needs to vomit.

I go to the living room, sit down and start to read the Sunday paper.

Ten minutes later, he is up, a wan smile on his face.

"I feel better," he says.

But he stays near that bucket for a good while.

Come, my people, enter your chambers, /and shut your doors behind you; /hide yourselves for a little while /until the wrath is past. Isaiah 26:20

Flustered

He was flustered. The company—a couple newly moved in next door—had just arrived. They were handing their coats to his wife, and he wanted to greet them.

But the baby was fussing, and the bottle was leaking all over his shirt.

He stood, setting the 14-month-old carefully down on the couch, and started for the other room.

Through the fog of his confusion, irritation and embarrassment, he heard the baby hitting the floor.

———————————————

At evening time, lo, terror! Isaiah 17:14

A (Select) List of Commands

Go over there.

Come over here.

Sit down.

Sit still.

Sit quietly.

Stand up.

Go outside and play.

Have fun.

Get some exercise.

See if your friend's home.

Take out the garbage.

Close the gate.

Get home on time.

Go to sleep.

Get up.

Get dressed.

Get going.

Listen.

Children, obey your parents in everything, for this is your acceptable duty in the Lord.
Colossians 3:20

Fathers and Sons

My father saw his 50-year-old father leave early mornings for his job loading box cars during the depths of the Depression. Grandpa took two long bus rides across the length of the city just to get to the yards.

I saw my father put on the uniform of a policeman for 33 years. When he'd come home, he'd wrap his gun and holster belt into a neat ball and store them in a locked drawer.

My son sees—what?

My briefcase? My story in the newspaper? Me on the telephone, talking to the office?

What will he recall of me when he looks back? What stories will he tell his son?

_____

*The righteous walk in integrity— /happy are
the children who follow them! Proverbs 20:7*

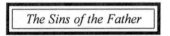

The Sins of the Father

He's not perfect. He's not close to perfect. But the kids love him. It is a wonder.

There are deep dark secrets that they don't know. Penny-ante stuff, really. Still, he wouldn't want them to know.

They wouldn't care.

They know the worst of it—his laziness, his utter lack of style, his problems at work.

They love him. And not just for his good parts. (There are good parts.)

He gave them life, and, in his imperfect way, he loves them. That counts for something.

He is the only father they have. The only father they want.

If we say that we have no sin, we deceive ourselves, and the truth is not in us. If we confess our sins, he who is faithful and just will forgive us our sins and cleanse us from all unrighteousness. 1 John 1:8-9

Protection

You try hard to protect your children.

You live in the suburbs. You make them wear their seat belts. You drive them where they have to go.

You teach them to avoid strangers. You teach them to watch out for con-artists. You get them ready for life in the world.

But now they're getting old enough to do things on their own.

Now they will have to start protecting themselves.

For wisdom will come into your heart, /and knowledge will be pleasant to your soul; /prudence will watch over you; /and understanding will guard you. Proverbs 2:10-11

Photographs on the Wall

They would sit in coffee shops and argue.

Now, she has rented an apartment a mile away and taken their two children with her.

Now, he sits in the large, empty house alone, waiting for the real estate agents to come through with prospective buyers.

On the walls are still the photographs of one big happy family.

———————————————

"Tear your clothes, and put on sack cloth."
2 Samuel 3:31

Let me tell you, children, about romance.

Your mother broke her leg. I got sick. We were both recovering when we met. Bingo! It was like a light going on when I saw her dancing with her leg in a cast up to her hip. Silly? Sure. Profoundly silly. So is love.

Sustain me with raisins, /refresh me with apples; /for I am faint with love. Song of Songs 2:5

Smart

He is cooking for the kids tonight.

He grills a steak and makes, by hit and miss, a sort of beef fried rice. He tells the kids to eat an apple, too, for a well-balanced meal.

The kids have two helpings of steak. They take a pass on the rice. They substitute an orange, cut in half, for the apple.

He bites into his own apple and finds it soft. The beef fried rice is soggy and tasteless.

They're pretty smart, his kids.

When the layer of dew lifted, there on the surface of the wilderness was a fine flaky substance, as fine as frost on the ground. When the Israelites saw it, they said to one another, "What is it?" For they did not know what it was. Moses said to them, "It is the bread that the LORD has given you to eat. Exodus 16:14-15

Coffee

What a pleasure coffee is—especially in the quiet of an evening.

For many years, I didn't drink much coffee at home. The kids were young. I was afraid they would spill the coffee on themselves. Besides, they were always on top of me, clinging to my legs, needing to be changed, wanting to be picked up, crying for a bottle, wanting—no, demanding—attention.

I barely had time to catch my breath, much less savor a hot cup of coffee.

Now, the kids are older. Now, as often as not, it's me who's trying to get their attention. Now they are involved in their own things and I've got time and space for a cup of coffee.

Excuse me while I take a sip.

Six years you shall sow your field, and six years you shall prune your vineyard, and a Sabbath of complete rest for the land, a sabbath for the LORD: you shall not sow your field or prune your vineyard. Leviticus 25:3-4

| *Fight* |

With a deafening roar, the earth between us splits, and we are standing now each on our distant cliff, separated from each other, it seems, by miles of open air.

She's to blame. She hurt me.

She's yelling something. I can't make it out across the chasm. Who cares?

I yell back. She doesn't hear, or doesn't pay attention.

This shouting makes the throat hoarse.

The canyon echoes our shouts as cacophony.

But it's so long a journey to the valley.

Above all, clothe yourselves with love, which binds everything together in perfect harmony. And let the peace of Christ rule in your hearts, to which indeed you were called in one body. Colossians 3:14-15

Cooking

There once was a father from Broadhurst

Whose cooking made kids and wife, all, curse.

So to restaurants they'd troop

For meat loaf and soup

'Cause mother's was, darn it, so much worse.

"How long will you torment me?" Job 19:2

> Time

What time is it?

How much time does it take to get there?

Do we have time?

What time does it start?

Remember the time . . . ?

Now concerning the times and the seasons,
brothers and sisters, you do not need to have
anything written to you. For you yourselves
know very well that the day of the Lord will
come like a thief in the night. 1 Thessalonians
5:1-2

School Play

As you hurry out the door to work, your wife says, "Don't forget. You son's school play is tonight."

"No problem," you say, "I've got a light day."

But, of course, it turns into a heavy day, and you're two hours late getting out of there.

On the way to the school you break several speed limits, carry out one illegal u-turn, give yourself indigestion, and arrive just in time.

The curtain is about to go up when your daughter says she's tired and wants to sit on your lap. It isn't long before she starts shivering and you know something's wrong.

You lean over and tell your wife you have to take the girl home, and then, carrying her over your shoulder, you try to tip-toe out of the assembly hall without causing too much disturbance.

At home, you daughter's limp with fever. You give her medicine and tuck her into bed. You realize how tired you are.

You're asleep before your son comes on stage at the start of the second act.

The human mind plans the way, /but the LORD directs the steps. Proverbs 16:9

Daughter Dead

There are no words to reach his grief.

At work, he goes through the motions. But the blackness is thick and rough and total.

There are yellow stabs of pain whenever he remembers her cock-eyed smile or the intense concentration that she brought to everything—from writing her name with the still-unfamiliar pencil to eating her bowl of Cheerios.

There are no words to reach him. Nothing can be heard over the animal howl in his skull.

I cry aloud to God, /aloud to God, that he might hear me. /In the day of my trouble I seek the Lord. Psalm 77:1-2

Antsy

I'm in an awkward time at work. My Big Project is coming to an end, and there are still lots of loose ends to tie up. But, after being constantly busy for months, I now find myself sitting at my desk with time to kill, waiting for my bosses to make their decisions.

I keep telling myself that, when I'm back in the regular swing of things, I'll recall these slow times with envy.

Maybe. But, for now, I'm antsy.

What do people gain from all the toil /at which they toil under the sun? /A generation goes, and a generation comes, /but the earth remains forever. Ecclesiastes 1:3-4

| *Abuse* |

When he was a child, he was beaten. Now he is a father, and he beats his kids.

He doesn't want to, but he knows no other way. The fury inside breaks out, like a wild animal.

He doesn't know how to stop. He doesn't stop.

He would beat himself if he could.

Like a city breached, without walls, /is one who lacks self-control. Proverbs 25:28

Fables

Slow and steady wins the race. That's how the fable goes. But in life, fast and brilliant is often victorious.

Cinderella got her prince. But don't look for too many waitresses to marry heirs.

Father knows best. But, in reality, I'm as confused as anyone.

Seek advice from every wise person and do not despise any useful counsel. Tobit 4:18

Model

The stern-faced man in the blue uniform wants me to buy a device to stop thieves from stealing my car—as if someone would want to. He's hard to avoid. He's on billboards along the highway and on the side of buses and at the entrances to the subway.

I see him. My children see him. As they ride together in the backseat of my car, they talk about the ad for "The Club."

My third-grader son says the ad is just a trick to get you to buy the thing. My daughter, two and a half years younger, agrees.

Their talk would seem terribly precocious, except that I know they're just parroting what I've said to them about the ad.

I'm their model. In this—and how much else?

Do not refrain from speaking at the proper moment, /and do not hide your wisdom; /For wisdom becomes known through speech. Sirach 4:23-24

Ticking

His sons run from one end of his cousin's apartment to the other, and back again, and back and forth. And he sits there at the dining room table, oblivious, telling a story about someone he knew in college who used to sleep on the floor of his dorm room.

His sons shout and yell and shriek in the aisles of the store. They're everywhere. And he stands there, explaining to an acquaintance why one particular brand of olive oil is superior to another.

It isn't until that night, when one of the boys—it doesn't matter which one—drops a cup of water while running out of the bathroom, that the father erupts.

Those with good sense are slow to anger, /and it is their glory to overlook an offense. /A king's anger is like the growling of a lion, /but his favor is like dew on the grass. Proverbs 19:11-12

Feminism

My daughter asks why there are no women playing basketball in the NBA, and why all of the presidents have been men.

My daughter is as bright and charming and lively and skillful as her brother.

It galls me that, even now, after so many changes in our society, she still faces limitations on her life because she isn't male.

I hope it galls her brother, too.

_____

Finally, beloved, whatever is true, whatever is honorable, whatever is just, whatever is pure, whatever is pleasing, whatever is commendable, if there is any excellence and if there is anything worthy of praise, think about these things. Philippians 4:8

Mornings

Most weekday mornings, I leave for my exercise class while the rest of the family is asleep.

Before I go, I wake up my wife briefly to give her a kiss and say good-bye. Then, I look in on my children.

My daughter has usually thrown off her covers and is sprawled out on the bed in some weird (but apparently comfortable) contortion. My son, on the other hand, is most often burrowed under his blankets with only his blond hair—buzz-cut in the fashion of third-grade—to be seen.

They never see themselves this way. And they can't know the mix of gentle, aching, joyful feelings that I get, looking at them so small and still, and just beginning their lives.

Let me hear of your steadfast love in the morning, /for in you I put my trust. /Teach me the way I should go, /for to you I lift up my soul. Psalm 143:8

Odd

This odd day brings odd thoughts.

Leap year only comes every four years.

If you're lucky, you'll have 20 leap years in your life.

How many have you used up already?

_____

Stand by your agreement and attend to it, and grow old in your work. Sirach 11:20

The Meaning of Fatherhood: Part 2

It's easy to get hung up on the difficulties of being a father. You have to be strong. You have to be gentle. You have to be organized. You have to be responsible.

There are paybacks: You hold your daughter's small hand on the way to kindergarten. You see your son's intent look of concentration as he reads his book. One child touches you lightly on the cheek to see if you've fallen asleep in your chair. The other whispers a secret in your ear in words too soft to understand.

Is Ephraim my dear son? /Is he the child I delight in? /As often as I speak against him, /I still remember him. /Therefore I am deeply moved for him; /I will surely have mercy on him, says the LORD. Jeremiah 31:20

```
┌─────────────┐
│     TV      │
└─────────────┘
```

He watches too much TV. Everyone tells him that.

He watches baseball, and football, and basketball. He watches the news. He knows every show that's on each night, how they're good, and how they're not.

His kids watch too much TV, too. Each has a bedroom TV set so there's no fighting over what to watch.

Sometimes, it happens, everyone gathers in the living room to see a special show or an important game together.

That's good.

But the rest is not.

———————————

My sheep were scattered, they wandered over all the mountains and on every high hill; my sheep were scattered over all the face of the earth, with no one to search or seek for them. Ezekiel 34:6

To My Wife

Like the flight of two cranes, our life together has been not effortless, to be sure, but constantly and always beautiful and filled with grace.

I love you now more deeply than I ever have, and I look with great joy and hope to the continued deepening of that love over the rest of our lives.

I love you like the flower opening to the sun, like the grass loves the soil.

The fig tree puts forth its figs, /and the vines are in blossom; /they give forth fragrance. /Arise, my love, my fair one, and come away. Song of Songs 2:13

Voicemail II

"Hi, Dad. This is your son.

"Dad, when you pick us up at the babysitter's, can we go out for a hot dog? And then a movie?

"On second thought, let's just go home and have a cozy night, the whole family together.

"Please call back for further details.

"I love you."

Although I have much to write to you, I would rather not use paper and ink; instead I hope to come to you and talk with you face to face, so that our joy may be complete. 2 John 12

An Indoor Playground

The boys and girls scream. They shout. Everything is done at a loud pitch. Even the giggling.

I don't like these indoor playgrounds. It's like sitting inside a jet engine . . . and paying good money for the opportunity.

My kids like them, though, especially on a day in late winter after being cooped up for weeks.

They are little animals—stretching and jumping and sliding and swinging and climbing and tumbling and laughing big belly laughs.

And there's no chance that they'll bother the people downstairs.

Let the sea roar, and all that fills it; /the world and those who live in it. /Let the floods clap their hands; /let the hills sing together for joy.
Psalm 98:7-8

Parent-Teacher Conference

It is with stomach-churning dread that he moves his car through rush-hour traffic on the way to his daughter's school and his meeting with her teacher.

He knows what will be said: She is not working to her potential. She is day-dreaming. She can do better. She can do much better.

His wife will listen and nod. He will sit there stolidly, all the while churning inside.

His wife has tried. He has tried. His daughter has tried. But she just doesn't get it.

School, for her, is like some arcane game, the point of which she can't fathom—any more than he can fathom what to do to help her.

Trust in the LORD with all your heart, /and do not rely on your own insight. /In all your ways acknowledge him, /and he will make straight your paths. Proverbs 3:5-6

Life and Death

That thing from Jesus about giving up your life for someone else—you never really understood it. Until now.

Oh, you could understand—intellectually, at least—martyrdom, or a soldier jumping on a grenade to save his buddies.

Even after you were married, it was still more theoretical than anything. Your wife has never really been under any threat or danger, and, besides, she is an adult. She knows how to handle herself. You are as likely to need help from her as she is to need help from you.

But now you have kids, and it's not so far-fetched any more.

Now you can picture yourself jumping in front of a car to save them. You can see yourself doing this—not grudgingly, but, in a strange way, almost joyfully, cheerfully. Giving up your life so they could live—well, that would be okay.

No one has greater love than this, to lay down one's life for one's friends. John 15:13

Drink

Your son has ruined his life with drink. He has ruined his job, ruined his family.

Your daughter-in-law and your grandchildren live out on the coast. You never see them.

You never see your son except for those holidays when he can pull himself together and dry himself out enough to be presentable.

He never asks for money. He never asks for anything.

There is a look around the corners of his eyes. It is a look of loss and failure and confusion. He says nothing.

You want to give him answers. All he'll let you do is give him a hug. And he stands there stiff to receive it.

Like a moth in clothing or a worm in wood,
/sorrow gnaws at the human heart.
Proverbs 25:20

One of Those Days

We're on our way to the toy store to pick up a birthday present, and my five-year-old daughter, on the seat next to me, jabbers gaily about school.

But I'm in a funk, feeling alone and undervalued. It's been one of those days.

On the way home, she asks hesitantly, "Dad, when you become a teenager . . . do you get big breasts?" (This is apropos of nothing—except maybe the wall of Barbies at the store.)

"Well," I say, not sure what to say, "some girls get big breasts. Some medium-size ones, and some small ones. It's just like some people are tall and some are short."

She has no more questions.

But I'm left to wonder if my answer was good enough. I'll probably always wonder.

But we pray to God that you may not do anything wrong—not that we may appear to have met the test, but that you may do what is right, though we may seem to have failed. For we cannot do anything against the truth, but only for the truth. 2 Corinthians 13:7-8

A Father Is Also a Son

He's angry at his brothers and sisters, and mad at his parents.

He shouldn't have to deal with this now, he thinks. He's an adult with a good job and kids of his own already in high school.

But he's angry with the family he grew up in. He's just one of the crowd. He's not special. Everyone's the same.

They won't even notice that he's angry.

How long, O LORD? Will you forget me forever? /How long will you hide your face from me? /How long must I bear pain in my soul, /and have sorrow in my heart all day long? Psalm 13:1-2

A Gift Scorned

My son draws well. I want to find him a teacher to help him learn all the techniques. It'll be a good foundation. He won't have to learn his trade by trial and error, the way I did. He won't have to grope around.

I want to give my son something I never had.

But he doesn't want it.

———————————————

"Please accept my gift that is brought to you, because God has dealt graciously with me, and because I have everything I want."
Genesis 33:11

The Way It Works

This is the way fatherhood works.

(1) Kids are congenitally hard of hearing—unless you and your wife are talking about something you don't want them to know.

(2) Your kids will always be too busy to tell you how school went—until the phone rings and you're in the middle of a business call.

(3) Your kids won't be interested in your wise analysis of the causes of the Civil War—until you're in an intersection, trying to make a left-hand turn with some clunker of a car with a teenager (obviously too young to be driving) behind the wheel barreling right at you from the other lane. Then they'll demand to know—right now!

"So I say to you, Ask, and it will be given you; search, and you will find; knock, and the door will be opened for you." Luke 11:9

| All Right |

You don't like her friends. Some are nerdy. Others are far too cool.

You don't want her to be unpopular. But those flashy guys—you know that glint in their eyes. You were a teenage boy once yourself.

But what of her? Does she also have that glint in her eyes?

She's not a little girl any more. She's a woman, even if she's still in high school.

She will make her own choices. She has to find her own way, no matter how much advice you give her, no matter how much you want to help her.

She'll be all right, you hope. And you hold your breath.

How can young people keep their way pure?
/By guarding it according to your word.
Psalm 119:9

Fatherland: One

It is scary to think that the idea of father was perverted in Germany to bolster Adolf Hitler and the Nazi Party.

The "fatherland" became identified with the effort to subjugate other nations and wipe certain peoples—Jews, gypsies, homosexuals, the mentally retarded—off the face of the earth.

In this context, the fatherland was stern, proud and cruel.

It was an evil place.

It was not worthy of the title.

Malicious witnesses rise up; /they ask me about things I do not know. /They repay me evil for good; /my soul is forlorn. Psalm 35:11-12

Fatherland: Two

The real fatherland is a place where the mountains are like strong shoulders, keeping out the worst of the weather.

It has a rich soil, frequently watered by a light rain and fed by lavish sunlight. The rainbows are a smile in the sky.

Groves of trees along the river bank gird the plains like two strong arms giving a happy bear hug.

The breezes cool sweaty foreheads in summer. In fall, they gently glide leaves to earth.

The rippling of the river water is a lullaby, whispering, "I love you."

"You were in Eden, the garden of God."
Ezekiel 28:13

Out of My Hands

I'd like my son to be a college professor or an artist, an historian or a veterinarian.

I'd like my daughter to be a writer or a doctor, a social worker or a community organizer.

They listen to these suggestions. And then go their own ways.

So much for what I want.

————————————

You, then, that teach others, will you not teach yourself? Romans 2:21

A Mirror

The part of me that's prudish wants to write off St. Patrick's Day as an excuse for some people to drink too much, act rowdy and be proud of a place their ancestors fled.

I want to pretend I'm above all that.

But when I see the floats lining up for the downtown parade, I have to stop. I look into the smiling faces off all the people dressed in green. I see their red hair and blue eyes and fair skin.

I know them—each and every one of them.

These are my people. I am rooted in their songs, their poetry, their drinking, their boasting, their keening and their laughter.

"Do not press me to leave you /or to turn back from following you! /Where you go, I will go; /where you lodge, I will lodge; /your people shall be my people, and your God my God. Ruth 1:16

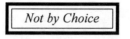

Not by Choice

One of my best friends is a seven-year-old boy who likes Power Rangers, *tae kwon do* and video games.

Well, he's really my son's good friend. Because of that, he's around our house a lot and goes along on many of our family outings and spends more time with me than my own friends.

This is something they never covered in those oh-so-long-ago parenting classes.

For better or worse, my children's friends are becoming my friends.

Some I like better than others. Some I find more courteous or attentive or interesting. Some get on my nerves.

But I don't have much of a say. I'm not the one making the choice.

—————————————

"You did not choose me but I chose you. And I appointed you to go and bear fruit, fruit that will last, so that the Father will give you whatever you ask him in my name." John 15:16

$$\boxed{\textit{Friends}}$$

In a restaurant, before my flight home, I sit reading a book until my attention is caught by a fifty-ish mother and her adult daughter, seated at the table across from me.

They are obviously good friends, laughing at small jokes, explaining to each other the details of clothing purchases (the feel of the cloth, the look of that particular shade), choosing from the menu with a discussion of the full range of options.

They are comfortable with each other. They lean toward each other when they speak so not a single word will be missed.

I watch and see, twenty years from now, my wife and our daughter—close, tight, enjoying each other's friendship.

"My dove, my perfect one, is the only one, /the darling of her mother, /flawless to her who bore her." Song of Songs 6:9

Punishment

You sit in judgment and find it awkward.

Here is your son. He snuck the small china Santa into his back park and brought it to school. But, on the way there, the back pack fell to the sidewalk and a chunk of Santa's leg is gone.

You son feels badly. He knows he's done wrong. He knows it can't be undone.

You're angry about the sneaking and the damage.

But as you look at your son, you also want to take him in your arms. You hate to see him feel so sad.

Instead, you must determine his punishment.

The earth, O Lord, is full of your steadfast love; /teach me your statutes. Psalm 119:64

| *The Son* |

His father was gay, although they didn't use that word then.

The son loved his father. He loved him for the way he listened, for the stories in his eyes—some sad, most happy.

He was the man who, to him, was just Dad.

————————————————

As a father has compassion for his children, /so the LORD has compassion for those who fear him. /For he knows how we were made. Psalm 103:13-14

The Father

The father always knew this day would come, but it was even more awkward than he imagined.

It was time to explain the birds and the bees, but the father was gay. What should he tell his pre-teen son about girls? About himself?

He talked about love and respect and responsibility and emotions. He talked about honesty and friendship. He talked about joy and loneliness and commitment.

That's how he started. The rest came as they went along.

For he created all things so that they might exist; /the generative forces of the world are wholesome, /and there is no destructive poison in them. Wisdom 1:14

> *China*

My five-year-old daughter drops a pile of china plates. Two break. She runs to her room, filled with embarrassment.

She cries and doesn't want to be seen. She feels like a fool. She feels like a baby.

I tell her it was an accident. It happens to everyone. My words don't get through. She is devastated.

I want to hug her to make it all better. But it is the gentle words of my wife that finally help her calm down and rejoin us at the table.

I feel badly—but not about the dishes.

A gentle tongue is a tree of life, /but perverseness in it breaks the spirit. Proverbs 15:4

Rock

You reach out your arms to your year-old daughter and say, "Come here. You can do it."

She wants to. She'd like to. She trusts you.

She lets go of the couch and promptly falls, banging her chin on the coffee table and cutting her lip.

She wails.

You pick her up, console her and say, "That's okay. That's okay. We'll try another time."

She calms down and holds you tight like a rock of love.

And you know your love is that solid.

Love bears all things, believes all things, hopes all things, endures all things. 1 Corinthians 13:7

Missing Them Already

In the car, the kids flood him with questions and comments and observations and ideas.

It gets to be hard work coming up with answers and responses, but he tries not to let it bother him.

He likes being with the kids. He likes it that they are so curious. And he loves that they want to talk to him.

He knows they won't be around forever. He knows they'll be grown someday and living somewhere else, and he'll be riding in his car alone.

He misses them already.

"As for me, if I am bereaved of my children, I am bereaved." Genesis 43:14

| Baseball Mitt |

You are repairing your first-baseman's glove, for only the second time in your life.

You were nine when you got it. Dwight Eisenhower was president. You were 19 and in college the first time you replaced its worn leather strips with new ones. Now, more than two decades later, you are fixing it again.

Your son, soon to be nine himself, has discovered the joys of playing catch—with you. He's still learning, but his throws are strong enough to strain the age-weakened replacement leather strips. Some have broken.

So, here you are, fixing the mitt again.

As you thread the new leather strips into the old holes, the dirt of many baseball fields falls onto the table in front of you.

For a thousand years in your sight /are like yesterday when it is past. Psalm 90:4

Wildly Successful

I read of this lawyer who bills his clients for about 5,000 hours a year. He explains he works 16 hours a day at least six days a week.

He makes huge amounts of money. His photo is on the front page. He's in *Who's Who*. He's called "wildly successful."

I wonder if he's a wildly successful dad.

When goods increase, those who eat them increase; and what gain has their owner but to see them with his eyes? Ecclesiastes 5:11

> No

"No, you can't go out to play now. It's dark."

"No, you can't watch TV now. You've seen enough today."

"No, we can't go to McDonald's for supper. We ate out last night."

"No, you can't skip your bath tonight. You were playing football in the backyard all afternoon."

"No, I don't like saying, 'No.' I really don't."

"I reprove and discipline those whom I love."
Revelation 3:19

Powerless

His daughter flies in the door, crying. Through the front window, he can see her boyfriend's car driving away.

The door to her room slams, but he can still hear her sobbing.

"What's wrong, honey?" he asks through the closed door.

"I don't want to talk about it!"

"Did Steve say something? Or do something?"

"Dad! Leave me alone!"

"Is there anything I can do?"

"There's nothing you can do! Nothing!"

He walks back to his chair. Slowly.

He had never realized how powerless a father could be.

"I have heard many such things; /miserable comforters are you all. /Have windy words no limit? /Or what provokes you that you keep on talking?" Job 16:23

> *Working Late*

I have to call the babysitter again and tell her I'll
be late. At six o'clock she has to take the kids down
the street to another sitter's home. I'll get there as
soon as I can.

My son, almost nine, gets on the phone and
complains that I've been working late too much.

It's true. But what can I do?

I'll get there as soon as I can.

---

*All one's ways may be pure in one's own eyes,
/but the Lord weighs the spirit. /Commit your
work to the Lord, /and your plans will be
established. Proverbs 16:2-3*

Christening

It is a sacred moment.

Your baby boy is being baptized. He is entering a new life. Putting on a new garment. Joining the faithful.

But your attention strays.

Your other two kids have slipped away and are walking on a nearby pew. Your sport coat smells of spit-up. You can't remember if, when you put the roast in the oven for the post-christening party, you turned the heat on.

"Do you renounce Satan?" the deacon asks.

You snap out of your reverie, and, on behalf of your new son, you fairly shout, "I do!"

"Go therefore and make disciples of all nations, baptizing them in the name of the Father and of the Son and of the Holy Spirit, and teaching them to obey everything that I have commanded you. And remember, I am with you always, to the end of the age."
Matthew 28:19-20

April 1

> *April Fool's Day*

So what's the trick, he wants to know. What's the secret? How strong does he have to be? And how gentle? How well-behaved should his children be? And how spirited? How hard should they work? And how much help should he give them? How much is he to blame for their failures? And how much credit does he deserve for their successes?

He wants to know, but no one can tell him.

That's the trick.

I am giving you these instructions, Timothy, my child, in accordance with the prophecies made earlier about you, so that by following them you may fight the good fight, having faith and a good conscience. 1 Timothy 1:18-19

Bright Eyes

In the middle of the night, asleep on the cot in the shelter, under his layers of clothing, he dreams:

He sees a man in a short-sleeve shirt with five pens in the pocket.

The man is walking into the backyard where a barbecue is in progress.

Three children—two girls and a boy—run to him and hug his knees.

The man bends down to kiss them.

He remembers their bright eyes even now, so many years later.

As for me, I shall behold your face in righteousness; /when I awake I shall be satisfied, beholding your likeness. Psalm 17:15

It's So Easy

Walking to kindergarten in the rain with my daughter, I have to bend down to hear her talking, from underneath her umbrella, about her new clothes.

She gets a lot of hand-me-downs. She has two cousins three years older than her, and they have a lot of very good clothes. So my daughter is always well-dressed.

But she doesn't get to pick out her clothes at a store very often.

So, last night, we went shopping, and she selected a dress and a pair of shorts and, as she says, "a silky t-shirt."

This is what she is telling me about again this morning as I bend down in the rain to hear her.

Sometimes fathering is so easy.

"Is there anyone among you who, if your child asks for a fish, will give a snake instead of a fish? Or if the child asks for an egg, will give a scorpion?" Luke 11:11-12

A Wonderment

It was, if you will, a minor miracle.

I'd read my children a bedtime story and was getting ready to put them to bed when they remembered that they hadn't yet had a bedtime snack.

I was tired—Aren't I always tired?—and didn't want to take the extra time. But they begged.

Suddenly, I got a bright idea. "Okay," I said to them. "You can have a snack if you promise to go to bed on your own when you're done."

"We promise," they said together.

And they did.

Happy are those who find Wisdom, /and those who get understanding. Proverbs 3:13

What You Want

You walk in the door, home from work, drained.

All you want to do is to lay down, close your eyes and let the day ebb away.

All you want is silence and rest.

Instead, it's:

"Daddy! He took . . ."

"Dear! The dishwasher. . ."

"Daddy! I broke. . ."

---

*"When they have a dispute, they come to me
and I decide between one person and another."
Exodus 18:16*

A Name for Fairness

My daughter is getting a name for fairness.

At kindergarten, she's quick to alert the teacher when things aren't right—such as when another girl sneaks to the front of the line.

At home, she asks if there are any women priests. When she's told there aren't, she says, "That's not fair!" And she means it.

Her box of cough drops is almost empty. She couldn't help sharing them with her friends. It was only fair.

Fairness is a good virtue, but sometimes a frustrating one.

Is any way unfair? Is it not your ways that are unfair? Ezekiel 18:25

They're Just Kids

You go to your son's house for dinner.

The grandkids are excited, and you are always, in some degree, amazed at these little people. They are your reach into the future. They are so alive!

Alas, too alive.

They're too loud, running through the house a foot above the floor, yelling, crying, shouting, singing.

Even when they sit still—in front of the TV— they put the sound on too loud.

How can you savor their wonder and beauty when they put your nerves on edge?

There are doubtless many different kinds of sounds in the world, and nothing is without sound. 1 Corinthians 14:10

Dad Can't Be Sick

It doesn't register with the kids that I'm sick.

It's not that they're loud or unusually obnoxious. It's just that they offer me none of the tender loving care that my wife and I lavish on them when they're ill.

They do come into the bedroom to see me, but they don't ask how I feel. They want me to read them a book.

Okay, why not?

Dad can't be sick. I'm the one who can fix any problem, answer any question, move any mountain, if need be, for them.

I'm a god of their universe.

———————————

For who is God except the LORD? /And who is a rock besides our God?— /the God who girded me with strength, /and made my way safe.
Psalm 18:31-32

April 9

| Inheritance |

My daughter and son, what will you inherit from me?

A world where people are afraid of each other. Yes, but also a goofy, loopy place where love happens.

Too many dusty shelves of books and too many boxes of files. Yes, but also the 1893 Indian-head penny that my grandmother from Ireland saved on a string around her neck.

My rageful shouts when I'm tired and stressed and feeling low. Yes, but also the feel of my soft, firm shoulder and my arms around you as I carry you in from the car.

And because you are children, God has sent the Spirit of his Son into our hearts, crying, "Abba! Father!" So you are no longer a slave but a child, and if a child then also an heir, through God. Galations 4:6-7

Middle-Age Temptation

You reach a certain age and rebel against the number.

You'll never play small forward in the NBA or be president of a Fortune 500 company. You'll never own a house without a mortgage or a leaky roof.

But, damn it, you're not dead yet.

You dye your hair. You grow a moustache. You buy clothes for the first time in decades with a concern for the latest styles. You get a fancy car. You lose weight.

And the young girls at the office look oh-so-sweet.

Blessed is anyone who endures temptation.
Such a one has stood the test and will receive
the crown of life that the Lord has promised to
those who love him. James 1:12

Forgiveness

After having to work late two nights in a row, I promise my kids I'll be on time tonight. It's my wife's work night, and I have to get them at the babysitter's. There is some special homework we're going to do, and then we'll have some quiet time together before bed.

But, again, an unexpected assignment arrives. I call to warn them I'll be late. Later, they call me. Then, I call them again. Finally, I can call to say I'm on my way.

Outside, I try to grab a taxi. It'll be expensive, but it's raining and I'm in a hurry.

But I can't find a cab and end up taking the subway. I walk—half jog—the mile home from the station.

When I get to the babysitter's, out of breath, the kids run to me and give me a hug.

They forgive me.

I had said in my alarm, /"I am driven far from your sight." /But you heard my supplications /when I cried out to your for help. Psalm 31:22

He is risen!

We go to church in our finery, celebrating after 40 days of fast and prayer.

He is risen!

The children scramble around the backyard, searching for plastic eggs filled with raisins, M&Ms and pennies.

He is risen!

The branches of trees begin to bud. It is spring again.

He is risen!

Set me as a seal upon your heart, /as a seal upon your arm; /for love is strong as death, /passion fierce as the grave. Song of Songs 8:6

Getting Ahead

He didn't win an award this year.

He didn't get a huge raise.

Other men and women, younger than he, got promoted ahead of him.

He doesn't have his own parking space. He has no corner office.

The other night, he wasn't invited to a many-hours-long strategy session at which the future direction of his firm was determined.

He was at home, putting his kids to bed.

For this slight momentary affliction is preparing us for an eternal weight of glory beyond all measure, because we look not at what can be seen but at what cannot be seen; for what can be seen is temporary, but what cannot be seen is eternal. 2 Corinthians 4:17-18

The Body

His legs are still strong and solidly muscled. His eyes are still clear. His beard is getting grey, but that's all right. He thinks it makes him look distinguished.

His paunch is what bothers him. He'd rather not think about it. Too many cheeseburgers. Too much fetuccini alfredo.

At the last turn of the century, a paunch like his was a sign of wealth.

He'd just as soon be a little poorer.

Sweet is the sleep of laborers, whether they eat little or much; but the surfeit of the rich will not let them sleep. Ecclesiastes 5:12

The Small Frame

On the wall of his office, amid the diplomas and photographs of politicians and entertainers he has worked with, is a small frame. Under the glass of the frame is the yellowed telegram that his mother received, notifying her of her husband's death in Korea. Three months later, their son was born. For that son, this now-brittle paper has come to symbolize his father. More than the blurry photos of a baby-faced soldier with a thin moustache, this paper has been, for him, the embodiment of the dad he never knew.

It is the hole in his life that will never heal.

Even these may forget, /yet I will not forget you. Isaiah 49:15

Exercise

It's Sunday afternoon, and we've finished a big mid-day meal and decide to walk to the lake. That is, my wife and I have decided.

The kids sort of like the idea, but not the walking part.

"Why can't we drive there?"

"It's only a mile away, and, besides, the whole point is to get some exercise," we explain firmly.

But they don't want to listen. And all the way there they complain.

We arrive at the beach and the kids run off, smiling widely, to swing and play on the other playground equipment and dig in the sand.

We are there maybe 45 minutes, and then it's time to head home.

And time for the kids to start complaining again. It's their form of exercise.

For the LORD had said to Moses, "Say to the Israelites, 'You are a stiff-necked people.'"
Exodus 33:5

Let's Talk about Sex

My 8-year-old son hears a fragment of a tune from the radio of a passing car and tells me the song is: "Let's Talk about Sex."

He and his 5-year-old sister are very curious about sex. They sense its mystery and power. They also sense how unsettling it can be.

They want to know. But they don't want to know.

My wife and I try to be straight-forward in dealing with their questions and comments. We don't want them to think that sex is dirty. We talk about love and happiness and sharing, but we're still pretty vague.

What are we going to do when they're teenagers?

My child, eat honey, for it is good, /and the drippings of the honeycomb are sweet to your taste. /Know that wisdom is such to your soul; /if you find it, you will find a future, /and your hope will not be cut off. Proverbs 24:13-14

Again

He is angry at her. Again.

She is too busy. Too tired. Too distracted by the kids. Too involved in her work. Too efficient.

Again.

He cannot find the words. He doesn't know how to start the conversation. He's tongue-tied. He stews.

This isn't how he expected it to be.

Therefore a man leaves his father and his mother and clings to his wife, and they become one flesh. Genesis 2:24

> One Thing at a Time

I can do only one thing at a time. But, oh, what wonderful things!

I can kiss my daughter's bruised finger and make it better.

I can read my son's homework and give him praise.

I can take the two kids to a hot dog stand, sit back and listen to their conversation.

I can touch my son's hair as he sleeps, as I used to touch his all-but-bald head when he was a sleeping baby.

I can compliment my daughter on her outfit and observe her sheepishly proud smile.

I can listen to my son read from one of his books.

I can lift the two kids up together and dance to an Aretha Franklin record. (But not for much longer.)

I can kiss my wife and forget the kids even exist.

I have seen the business that God has given to everyone to be busy with. He has made everything suitable for its time. Ecclesiastes 3:10-11

My Daughter's Birthday

Today is my daughter's birthday. She will wear a special dress today. She will smile her big-eyed, six-year-old smile today. We will take her to dinner—her brother, her mother and I. We will take her to the movie she wants to see. We will go swimming together.

She is happy with all the attention.

We're happy she's one of us.

And when I was born, I began to breathe the common air, /and fell upon the kindred earth; /my first sound was a cry, as is true of all. /I was nursed with care in swaddling cloths.
Wisdom 7:3-4

He Tells Himself

He doesn't call his grown daughter, now out on her own.

It's her responsibility to call him, he tells himself. He is, after all, her father. She owes him regular phone calls. She owes him respect.

He shouldn't have to sit here day after day waiting for her to call, he tells himself. She's not being a good daughter.

He was a good father, he tells himself. Wasn't he?

For you reap whatever you sow. Galatians 6:7

Yes and No

He says "yes" to his boss.

He says "yes" to his wife.

He says "yes" to his kids.

He says "no" to himself.

"As for you also, because of the blood of my covenant with you, /I will set your prisoners free from the waterless pit." Zechariah 9:11

Titles I

Dad

Daddy

Da

Pa

Papa

Poppa

Pop

Pappy

The Old Man

Father

They will call on my name, /and I will answer them. Zechariah 13:9

> Bingo

I bring my son to the art museum. I want to show him an El Greco painting. He wants to see the suits of armor.

I bring him to the baseball game. I want to show him Nolan Ryan. He wants to get a hot dog. And a Coke. And some nachos. And popcorn. And another hot dog.

I bring him to a musical revue of Fats Waller's songs. I want to show him the joy of the rhythms and the delight of the melodies. He dances in his seat, and he sings along.

Bingo.

O sing to the LORD a new song; /sing to the LORD, all the earth. /Sing to the LORD, bless his name; /tell of his salvation from day to day.
Psalm 96:1-2

No Sleep

It's one A.M. Your wife and kids are sleeping soundly. But you're wide awake.

You've just finished one big project, and you're glad to have it over . . . and such a success.

But you leave in the morning on an important business trip. You're nervous about flying and about carrying out your assignment when you get there.

Your heart is racing. And so is the dawn, coming your way.

"I am not at ease, nor am I quiet; /I have no past, but trouble comes." Job 3:26

At the Cemetery

He finds his father's sister's grave site. It's the family plot of her in-laws. There's a big stone cross with the family name at the base. A few flat gravestones are in the ground around the cross. None is hers.

It's been nine years since her burial. Will she ever have her own stone?

This is the first time he's visited.

His dad would be so disappointed.

Lead a life worthy of the calling to which you have been called, with all humility and patience, bearing with one another in love, making every effort to maintain the unity of the Spirit in the bond of peace. Ephesians 4:1-3

Funeral

"He was," the priest says, "a good father, a good husband, a good man."

What he doesn't say, but what everyone in the church can see, is that the widow is devastated.

She is young and shaken. She was oh so much in love with her husband, and now he is gone.

And their boy?

He looks out over the top of the pew with his three-year-old's eyes, wondering why he feels so bad.

My soul melts away for sorrow; /strengthen me according to your word. Psalm 119:28

Daydream

At church, when he was a boy, he'd daydream about the moment when he, the first baseman, would stretch far out with his mitt, and the ball, thrown by one of the other infielders, would slam into the pocket like a child scooped up in a father's arms, held safe, held secure, held forever.

_____

*"As the L*ORD* lives, not one hair of your son shall fall to the ground." 2 Samuel 14:11*

> *Garbage*

You found beer cans again in the kitchen garbage when you pulled the bag out to carry to the alley.

They weren't yours. They weren't your wife's.

You know it had to be your teenage son who left them. And you know you've got to confront him again.

What's going wrong?

_____

Even children make themselves known by their acts, /by whether what they do is pure and right. Proverbs 20:11

Talking about Children

A dinner party. Five couples around the table, one newly married.

"We're thinking about having kids," the new husband says.

The other men respond.

"Kiss your sleep good-bye."

"Kids enrich your life so much. They're hard work, but, gee, when I get to the babysitter's after work and ring the bell, I can hear the pitter-patter of their feet on the floor as they run to open the door to greet me."

"It's amazing to think that, for these little guys, you're the most important person in the world."

"I never thought I'd enjoy changing diapers so much."

See what love the Father has given us, that we should be called children of God; and that is what we are. 1 John 3:1

> *May Day*

The new leaves on the trees whisper in the wind. The sun, a long lost friend, returns. The grass grows thick and green. Even the cement sidewalk looks good.

You can remember such days when you were eight.

You can remember the mix of joy and hope in your blood.

It's still there on a spring day like today.

For now the winter is past, /the rain is over and gone. /The flowers appear on the earth; /the time of singing has come, /and the voice of the turtledove /is heard in our land. Song of Songs 2:11-12

Illness

The father knows that the illness will kill the boy. Already, the boy's body is twisted and turned in on itself.

He is only four and will get no older.

The boy cannot talk, except in grunts. He cannot control his bowels.

The father picks him up in his arms and looks into the boy's eyes. And smiles.

Despite the pain, the father is happy to have the chance to love his son.

Guard me as the apple of the eye; /hide me in the shadow of your wing. Psalm 17:8

Too Much Hitting

My eight-year-old son is at a school dance, and, of course, he isn't dancing. He's roaming along the edges of the gym with a pack of other third-grade boys, stopping every once in a while to give a ninja kick or turn a somersault.

Now his group of boys is swooping past a smaller group of girls who, in their turn, come swooping back. And then my son is slamming one of the girls hard on the shoulders, and she is slamming back.

They're laughing, sort of. And the books all say that this is normal developmental stuff. But I don't care. I don't want him to get the idea that he can beat on anyone, particularly girls. There's too much hitting in the world as it is.

I pull him off to the side and sit him down. His pack of friends sit down together a few feet away, waiting for his release. He doesn't complain . . . too much.

"Blessed are the peacemakers, for they will be called children of God." Matthew 5:9

A Glimpse

Every once in a while, he catches a glimpse of his true self. It's there somewhere, somewhere deep inside him.

This true self is less tense, less in need of being in control. This self is weaker, but not weak. More flexible, more quick to laugh . . . and to cry. His true self enthuses, exults, squeals with delight. Has emotions. Feels.

Every once in a while, he sees this true self. But only for a moment.

Never for more than a single moment.

The beginning of wisdom is this: Get wisdom, /and whatever else you get, get insight. /Prize her highly, and she will exalt you; /she will honor you if you embrace her. Proverbs 4:7-8

May 5

Pete says: "At work, I feel like an undercover agent. It's hard. My bosses are so focused on profits and promotions. Some are as cut-throat as you can get. I feel like the odd man out."

George says: "My baby died nine months ago, and I still cry. I'm so confused. I hurt so much. That's all I can say."

Steve says: "I was dating this girl. She had a beautiful face. But that was it. I didn't feel anything. I knew something was wrong when I met her brother and found him more attractive than her. I thought to myself: This isn't the way it's supposed to be; I don't want this."

_____

"Come to me, all you that are weary and are carrying heavy burdens, and I will give you rest." Matthew 11:28

Men's Retreat: Day 2

John says: "When my mother died, my father ran away and consoled himself with another woman. My brother and I were left to fend for ourselves."

Bill says: "My wife and I went through a rough period. There were times I didn't want to be in the same room with her."

Frank says: "I didn't know what to do with my daughter. She was so willful."

Sid says: "I could never make the jump shot."

Thank God for Sid.

"I came so that they might have life, and have it more abundantly." John 10:10

Sweet Dreams

"Get back in bed."

It's one of those nights when the kids just won't go to sleep. All my wife and I want is some time together in front of the TV—no great romantic evening, but the Monday Night Football game does look mildly interesting. (It's already the second quarter, and our side's down by a touchdown.)

But this is one of those nights when the kids aren't tired enough, or they're too tired.

They keep sneaking out of their bedrooms, hiding behind the furniture, conspiring together in loud whispers, all agiggle.

All we want to do is veg out, but, time and again, we have to get up to chase the kids back to their rooms.

They'd be cute, if they weren't making us so damned angry.

When you are disturbed, do not sin; /ponder it on your beds, and be silent. Psalm 4:4

The Toast

The grass gets cut. The kids are picked up at school. The garbage is taken out. The shopping is done. Dinner is served. The rug is vacuumed. Games are put away. The dirty dishes get washed, the tub gets scoured. Books are read, prayers are said, the children are tucked into bed.

Then—and only then—the glasses are filled with wine. And a toast is drunk to the end of another day.

I would lead you and bring you /into the house of my mother, /and into the chamber of the one who bore me. /I would give you spiced wine to drink, /the juice of my pomegranates. Song of Songs 8:2

The Meaning of Fatherhood: Part 3

Here he is now, the new father, holding his day-old son in his arms.

He smiles broadly, but inside he's confused. He never had a father. And now he's expected to be one.

Does a father have to take care of the toilet-training?

What about spanking? And the birds and the bees? And picking out a career?

He's a happy new father, but also a scared one.

"You are my son; /today I have begotten you."
Psalm 2:7

A Father Like That

His daughter brings home this guy who is loud and gross and opinionated and wears this thin, little moustache.

He can't understand why his daughter is wasting her time on this guy.

His daughter, he believes, should have the perfect boyfriend—someone handsome, successful, polite, attentive, gentle, experienced, wise, healthy, intelligent, joyful, mechanically inclined, clever . . .

Then he stops himself with a laugh.

She should have a father like that.

How beautiful upon the mountains /are the feet of the messenger who announces peace, /who brings good news, /who announces salutation, /who says to Zion, "Your God reigns." Isaiah 52:7

Three Generations

The grandson didn't want to be there.

The nursing home smelled bad. Everyone was old. They didn't look right.

His grandfather acted weird, like he was asleep and awake at the same time. His father acted weird, too, like he was Grandpa's father.

That made the grandfather and the grandson the same somehow—both dependent on the one man.

The grandson didn't want to be there.

"I will establish my covenant between me and you, and your offspring after you throughout their generations, for an everlasting covenant, to be God to you and your offspring after you."
Genesis 17:7

The Whisper

It comes at such unlikely moments—like the present-opening part of a five-year-old's birthday party.

It comes sometimes as you do the dishes or vacuum the rug.

You hear it—half hear it really—in the middle of the night.

It's that scratch voice not quite audible under the noise of the television set. It's deep within the hum of the refrigerator.

You hear it at odd moments, but never loud or clearly enough to make out the words.

It's the whisper of how it all fits together.

"Surely the Lord is in this place—and I did not know it!" Genesis 28:16

Housework

There once was a Dad from New York

Whose children refused to do housework.

He grounded them all,

Kept them home from the mall.

Whining, they called him an old dork.

---

*Pay to all what is due them—taxes to whom
taxes are due, revenue to whom revenue is due,
respect to whom respect is due, honor to whom
honor is due. Romans 13:7*

Miscarriage

He holds his sobbing wife.

He is so low, he cannot envision tomorrow.

He can only think of the boy who would have run around in the backyard, and learned to ride a bicycle, and gone on his first date, and graduated from college, and gotten a job that paid good money, and fallen in love with a good woman, and married, and fathered his own child.

He wishes he could have held that boy, just once, in his arms.

A voice is heard in Ramah, /lamentation and bitter weeping. /Rachel is weeping for her children; /she refuses to be comforted for her children, /because they are no more. Jeremiah 31:15

| Voicemail III |

"Hi, Dad.

"Um, I'm calling, um . . . I just want to say: It's Saturday. You're out with Mom. I love you.

"Bye."

Beloved, I pray that all may go well with you and that you may be in good health, just as it is well with your soul. 3 John 2

Across Town

Your daughter takes the bus across town to the good school in the bad neighborhood.

You are glad she is learning how to get around. You are happy she is meeting kids from other backgrounds.

This will enrich her, you tell yourself. Her personality will broaden. She will be comfortable in strange situations. She will be less frightened of the unknown.

But each afternoon you call to make sure she's gotten home all right.

If I take the wings of the morning /and settle at the farthest limits of the sea, /even there your hand shall lead me, /and your right hand shall hold me fast. Psalm 139:9-10

Weights

He is weighed down by his children and by his job and by his wife's demands and by what he was taught and by what he expects of himself and by what he fears and by his bills and by his errands and by his football team's loss.

She wants to lift those weights off his shoulders, but he fights her off.

"I'm so used to them," he says. "I'd be uncomfortable without them."

"Take my yoke upon you, and learn from me; for I am gentle and humble in heart, and you will find rest for your souls. For my yoke is easy, and my burden is light." Matthew 11:29-30

Fine Dining

I'm taking the kids out for pizza, and they're being snotty.

My daughter demands money for stickers. My son wants two personal pan pizzas for himself.

My daughter's mad that her brother got breadsticks and won't share them. He's upset that she got a prize with her meal.

He wanted to be served first. She sticks her tongue out at him.

I get indigestion.

Better is a dinner of vegetables where love is / than a fatted ox and hatred with it. Proverbs 15:17

The Busy Family

My wife and I are just too busy. Something has to give.

I've got extra work that keeps me late at the office.

My wife's job, too, is more demanding right now.

There are weddings and parties and meetings and conferences to get to.

And then there are the kids' schedules: soccer, Brownies, play dates, competitions, movies.

We're the Busy Family.

Better is a handful with quiet /than two
handsful with toil, /and a chasing after wind.
Ecclesiastes 4:6

You Are There

Your daughter comes up to you. "Dad, my tooth is loose. It's going this and that way. See?"

You can't see because her hand is in the way, but you know what she means.

"Which tooth is it?" you ask. She points to one on the top in the front.

You take a wad of Kleenex to get a good hold on the tooth. It is hanging by a thread. You pull ever so softly, and it is free.

Your daughter smiles a new gap-tooth smile, and the two of you look at the tiny piece of her in the Kleenex.

She knows she's growing up. And so do you.

And you are there.

And as for me, this is my covenant with them, says the Lord; my spirit that is upon you, and my words that I have put in your mouth, shall not depart out of your mouth, or out of the mouths of your children, or out of the mouths of your children's children, says the Lord, from now on and forever. Isaiah 59:21

The end of the day.

I'm empty.

I have nothing to give, no energy to do anything.

Please let my wife and kids be asleep.

---

*I have passed out of mind like one who is
dead; /I have become like a broken vessel.
Psalm 31:12*

And When I Die

I want to be buried with a big headstone over me.

I want the stone to be distinctive. I want its shape to be sharply cut, and its surface smoothly polished.

I want my full name on the stone, and the dates of my birth and my death.

I want some special words on the stone. I don't know what they should be.

And I want my wife and kids to come from time to time.

They won't have to pray. Or cry.

I just want them to come and touch the stone on a bright crisp autumn day when the leaves are falling and the snow is soon to come.

But we do not want you to be uninformed, brothers and sisters, about those who have died, so that you may not grieve as others do who have no hope. 1 Thessalonians 4:13

> *Chaos*

He watched the grade school dance and thought about chaos.

Song after song was played, but—fast or slow, rap or rock—the music was less an organizing principle than a sort of background hum to the hundred or so children in the gym. The basketball court, ostensibly a "dance" floor, was a feast of random movement.

True, every once in a while some kids here and there, even large groups of kids, would stop what they were doing and actually dance a few steps. But, for every dancer, there were 4 or 5 watchers, talkers, pop drinkers, gigglers, runners, ninja kickers, popcorn eaters, laughers, cartwheelers, ring-pop suckers and smilers.

There was a lot of smiling going on. The kids liked the chaos. They didn't find it scary or unnerving.

For them, it was exhilarating.

"Let the little children come to me, and do not stop them; for it is to such as these that the kingdom of God belongs. Truly I tell you, whoever does not receive the kingdom of God as a little child will never enter it." Luke 18:16-17

Scrambled Eggs

My eight-year-old son now makes scrambled eggs on his own. Well, almost on his own. Today, at the restaurant, he ate more pieces of pizza than I did.

When he does such things, he looks at me out of the side of his eyes with a knowing look that seems to say, "Isn't life great, Dad?"

As I watch him, I see myself growing up, remember what it was like for me, compare and contrast my childhood with his.

Yes, son, it certainly is.

I was daily his delight, /rejoicing before him always, /rejoicing in his inhabited world /and delighting in the human race. Proverbs 8:30-31

Why

Why are mothers afflicted with guilt? And fathers with anger?

Why are mothers taught to hug? And fathers to hand down judgments?

Why are mothers so filled with words? And fathers so inarticulate?

If then there is any encouragement in Christ, any consolation from love, any sharing in the Spirit, any compassion and sympathy, make my joy complete: be of the same mind, having the same love, being in full accord and of one mind. Philippians 2:1-2

A Love Story

He met her in Columbia.

They reached across race, language and culture to marry.

They raised three children. They laughed, argued, embraced, fought, cried and just sat with each other across the kitchen table.

He has never forgotten the way she looked that afternoon, waiting in the convent garden for the wedding to begin.

————————————————

I am black and beautiful /O daughters of Jerusalem, /like the tents of Kedar /like the curtains of Solomon. Song of Songs 1:5

Golden Evening

My wife is in the Canadian Rockies on a week's vacation with a girlfriend. I'm at home, off from work, watching the kids and taking it easy.

After a week of cold days, it is suddenly warm but not too hot. The kids jibber-jabber in the backyard, rolling in the grass, playing games and talking to two new-born ducklings on loan from their school for the weekend.

The green of the grass is refreshing. As the sun moves toward setting, I can almost feel the grass—and my children—grow.

I have nowhere to go. I'm where I belong.

See, now is the acceptable time; see, now is the day of salvation. 2 Corinthians 6:2

Not an Epidemic

My daughter's leg hurts. Then her shoulder.

My son has a headache. He needs a glass of water. He has to go to the bathroom three times in ten minutes.

No, this isn't an epidemic. Just bedtime.

I will not give sleep to my eyes /or slumber to my eyelids, /until I find a place for the LORD.
Psalm 132:4-5

How to Feel

He left the house one day and didn't come back.

He's living somewhere downtown. He mails a check twice a month. He won't take his wife's calls at work. He dodges her when she tries to see him.

The kids don't know how to feel.

It's all right, an uncle tells them, to be mad at Daddy.

From noon on, darkness came over the whole land until three in the afternoon. And about three o'clock Jesus cried with a loud voice, "Eli Eli, lema sabachthani?" that is, "My God, my God, why have you forsaken me?" Matthew 27:45-46

Singing

I take my son and his friend to church with me.

This is a dicey proposition, but they surprise me. Instead of inciting each other to act up, they help each other keep calm and quiet.

They even sing along with the hymns—in a nine-year-old sort of way.

One song I particularly like, and I sing out the chorus with full voice.

Each time I do, my son's friend turns his head sharply to look up at me, as if examining an odd artifact from a far distant civilization.

I sing even louder. And smile to myself.

Are any among you suffering? They should pray. Are any cheerful? They should sing songs of praise. James 5:13

| Errands |

He's running errands on a weekday. His kids are in school. His wife is at work.

He comes out of yet another store after yet another frustrating attempt to find the exact sort of metal brace he needs to fix the back porch.

Suddenly—in the aftermath of a light spring rain—he smells the green leaves of the trees, rich with sap and life. And he feels the brisk cool breeze that gives a piquant edge to the sweet perfume of the trees.

And he breathes in the goodness of creation.

"Martha, Martha you are worried and distracted by many things; there is need of only one thing." Luke 10:41-42

Immortality and Mortality

My 8-year-old son is happy. Last night, we sat together and looked through some art books. Tonight, we're to do it again.

He points out two that he likes especially. One is a collection of Michelangelo's work, another of Leonardo da Vinci.

He tells me, "Dad, when you die, I'm going to take all your art books."

He sits down next to me on the couch and adds tenderly, "Of course, I hope it's not for a long time— like, maybe, 17 years."

The days of our life are seventy years, /or
perhaps eighty, if we are strong. Psalm 90:10

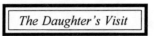

The Daughter's Visit

She can still make him smile.

When she hasn't been over, he broods. He worries abut his various illnesses. He mourns his wife. He chews over the bitterness of his old job.

But when his little girl visits—now a big, strapping, wide-smiled, deep-throated, bright-eyed giant of a woman—he changes.

They go to the store, to the movies, out to eat together.

And, for days after, he can't stop smiling.

———————————————

"Let the little children come to me; do not stop them; for it is to such as these that the kingdom of God belongs." Mark 10:14

At the Library

On the library computer, I show off for my eight-year-old son, but he keeps pace with me, noticing everything I do.

I call up the titles I'm looking for and see if they're available at this branch or one of the others.

"You forgot the second one on the list," my son says. He's right.

When I'm done he wants me to check on a book for him. We do that, and then go to the stacks to find it.

"JUV GV11.A2 . . . ," I say, half to myself as I look along the stacks.

I show my son how to find that number, but when we get to the spot, the book isn't there—even though it's supposed to be.

So much for showing off.

"What you know, I also know." Job 13:2

Envy

In your deepest heart, you know you're jealous of your children.

They are fresh and full of life, full of hope and expectation. You feel empty so often.

They have the vast field of life before them. No option is yet blocked for them. Your aims now are narrow, mundane. You have learned your limits.

They are excited at the mystery of life. You are just trying to get by.

They don't know how rich they are. You realize how poor you have become.

Nor will I travel in the company of sickly envy,
for envy does not associate with wisdom.
Wisdom 6:23

Saturday Night

My wife and I sit in the back yard near the cooling-down Weber grill, drinking coffee and talking about the sunset, the smell in the basement drain, the ivy climbing the corner of the garage, her mother, my mother, a man I met at work, our children running in and out of the graduation party next door, the job she's been offered, our Colorado vacation two months away, an odd pattern of clouds, the colleges our children will attend a decade from now, the way the grass is cut, the possible purchase of a saw, the schedule for Sunday, something our daughter said at the store, something our son said in the car, our old vacations before the kids, our thoughts about moving, the front porch's need for paint and the fact that it's time to call the kids in for bed.

"Six days you shall work, but on the seventh day you shall rest." Exodus 34:21

June 6

> ### The Answer, Please

You are taking out the garbage to the alley in the dark and stumble across your son and his girlfriend necking on the chaise lounge.

Do you . . .

(a) Give them a lecture on the need for responsibility in sex?

(b) Say "hi" and keep on walking?

(c) Whistle a happy tune and pretend you don't see them?

The answer, please.

———————————————

Remember the days of old, /consider the years long past; /ask your father, and he will inform you; /your elders, and they will tell you.
Deuteronomy 32:7

F-A-T-H-E-R

F is for how Fat I'm getting.

A is for how Addled I can be.

T is for the Toys I like to play with.

H is for the Hole I have in my shoe.

E is for the Extra-strength antacids that I chew.

R is for the Rest of my short-comings.

Put them all together, and they spell: "I'm just an imperfect, error-prone, often clumsy, sometimes grouchy, frequently tired, usually sloppy, occasionally embarrassing, all-too-human (but, kids, I love being your) FATHER."

"Do not look on his appearance or on the height of his stature, because I have rejected him; for the LORD does not see as mortals see; they look on the outward appearances, but the LORD looks on the hearts. 1 Samuel 16:7

Calling

The old man dials his son. He sits at the table, waiting. He hears the ringing. He waits.

He's not sure he should call. After all, it's not an emergency. It's just that he thought this morning of his wife, dead now three years, and he's been blue ever since.

His son's probably busy. He always sounds busy at the office.

The old man moved to hang up the phone, but his son picks up.

"Hi, Dad!" the son says. "It's great to hear from you."

Those who honor their father will have joy in their own children, /and when they pray they will be heard. Sirach 3:5

Incense

We wait for the kindergarten celebration. We sit on tiny chairs and wait for our kids to walk out on stage to be honored for completing their first year of "real" school.

A younger brother is holding two big silver balloons. One balloon gets away from him. He reaches for it. The other floats loose too.

The two balloons ascend. We all watch.

The balloons seem to represent all the hopes and dreams we parents have for our kids. They are like incense, rising to heaven to ask God's blessing.

Who are these that fly like a cloud, and like doves to their windows? Isaiah 60:8

He Remembers

He remembers being six and sitting in a restaurant, just he and his father, eating hot dogs and talking.

He remembers being 15 and his father coming into his room to say he'd been over-reacting and let's talk about it.

He remembers being 29 and dressed in a tuxedo, standing a few feet from the altar and waiting for the wedding to start, his father gripping him tight in a bear hug and crying.

As you know, we dealt with each one of you like a father with his children, urging and encouraging you and pleading that you lead a life worthy of God, who calls you unto his own kingdom and glory. 1 Thessalonians 2:11

The Father Song

Go to work, come back home.

Teach the children not to roam.

Do-whah, do-whah.

Play games, let them win.

Explain why fish should need a fin.

Do-whah, do-whah.

Tuck them in, kiss them 'night.

Show them wrong, show them right.

Do-whah, do-whah.

Hold them, scold them

Soothe them, enfold them.

Do-whah, do-whah.

Let them love you, let them see you,

Warts and all, let them need you.

Do-whah, do-whah.

Love them, love their mother.

You're their dad, they have no other.

Do-whah, do-whah.

Let the word of Christ dwell in you richly;
teach and admonish one another in all wisdom;
and with gratitude in your hearts sing psalms,
hymns, and spiritual songs to God. And
whatever you do, in word or deed, do every-
thing in the name of the Lord Jesus, giving
thanks to God the Father through him.
Colossians 3:16-17

> *A Dream*

His son wants to give up the solid job he has now to go off to another city to chase a dream.

He's angry at the boy, frustrated. Can't he see reason?

Look at all he wants to give up. He's upsetting his family. He's risking his career. And for what?

To follow a dream.

The same dream his father abandoned so long ago.

I will pour out my spirit on all flesh; /your sons and your daughters shall prophesy, /your old men shall dream dreams, /and your young men shall see visions. Joel 2:28

| Routine |

His father is in the hospital again.

Again, he is having trouble with his heart.
Again, he is in for tests and some modifications in his
medications.

As usual, Dad can't wait to get out.

The scary thing is how routine all this has
become.

And Mom pretends nothing is happening.

---

*Turn to me and be gracious to me, /for I am
lonely and afflicted. /Relieve the troubles of my
heart, /and bring me out of my distress. Psalm
25:16-17*

| Unity |

It is so hot. I am limp as spoiled lettuce.

The kids have been stuck inside all day, clustering around the one window air conditioner. They're sapped by the humidity and at each other's throats.

We all feel caged, united in our discomfort.

It's not exactly the family unity I had in mind.

---

*How very good and pleasant it is /when kindred
live together in unity! Psalm 133:1*

Hands

On the way to the kitchen, you spot your infant son in his crib contemplating his hands.

He holds them up above his face and watches them twist and turn.

He is moving them, although he doesn't yet realize that.

He is smiling, too.

So are you.

"Ah, the smell of my son /is like the smell of a field that the LORD *has blessed. /May God give you the dew of heaven, /and the fatness of the earth, and plenty of grain and wine." Genesis 27:27-28*

Nightmares

My daughter had nightmares last night.

Was it because of the movie she saw yesterday about the mermaid and the man who fell in love?

Or was it because her friend's mother gave birth yesterday in a many-houred labor?

My daughter, young as she is, is a woman. In her are the mysteries of love and birth.

"When a woman is in labor, she has pain, because her hour has come. But when her child is born, she no longer remembers the anguish because of the joy of having brought a human being into the world." John 16:21

Catch

My son and I play catch.

He's getting pretty good at catching the ball. His arm has always been strong—if not always accurate.

I have to bend over, often, to catch his throws. My old mitt scoops up the ball when I can reach it. But I can't bend over as far or as easily as I could when I was younger.

I'm careful when I throw the ball to him.

Each time, I hold my breath until he gets his mitt up in time so the ball doesn't hit him in the face.

———————————————

To the weak I became weak, so that I might win the weak. 1 Corinthians 9:22

Getting Started

With the children gone to college, the house is quiet, and you aren't sure what to do with yourself.

But you can't wait to get started.

Surely goodness and mercy shall follow me /all the days of my life, /and I shall dwell in the house of the LORD /my whole life long. Psalm 23:6

Father's Day

Father's Day at the ball park. The home team hero hits a home run. His kids cheer. They hold up their fists in the air in triumph. They shout with unrestrained joy. Their eyes are bright with happiness.

This is how he always hoped it would be.

Father's Day at the ball park. The home team hero strikes out. His kids boo. They whine about being there. They hate baseball. They hate him.

This is how he always feared it would be.

Hope deferred makes the heart sick, /but a desire fulfilled is a tree of life. Proverbs 13:12

> ### Nose Ring

When his daughter got the ring in her nose, he made sure not to over-react.

After all, she was in college. It was her body. And it is the nature of youth to rebel.

Better a nose ring than drugs, or shop-lifting, or dropping out of school.

Still, every time he sees her with the ring in her nose, his own nose twitches. And he wonders that she does when she has a cold.

Maybe he'll ask her.

(But probably he won't.)

For wisdom is better than jewels, /and all that you may desire cannot compare with her. /I, wisdom, live with prudence, /and I attain knowledge and discretion. Proverbs 8:11-12

Scar

It's a small thing, really. But, whenever I see the scar on my son's knee, I cringe.

He was about 5, and he was rolling down a small slope near our house. His knee struck a sharp piece of metal in the tall grass. That's how the cut happened.

He didn't pay much attention. Kids often ignore small pains when they're having fun. But the cut was deep, and it left a deep scar.

The thing is that I was there when it happened. I saw him get up with blood on his knee. I looked at the wound as much as he would let me. But because he wasn't upset or in any obvious pain, I let him go back to his play.

His body was scarred, even as I watched.

I cringe when I think of all that is happening to form, shape—and yes, scar—him that I don't even notice.

Yet, O Lord, you are our Father; /we are the clay, and you are our potter; /we are all the work of your hand. Isaiah 64:8

An Open Book

He appeared on TV. It was one of those flukes—
a man on the street thing. But everyone saw him, and
everyone wanted to tell him about it. It was as if he
was suddenly a celebrity. Which, of course, he was, in
the way of the modern world.

His kids were less impressed.

Life is still an open book to them.

Dad on TV? Why not?

Dad as president? Sure.

Dad winning the Boston marathon? So what?

He asks them if they'd like to go for a bike ride.

"Yesssssssss," they reply.

---

*Vanity of vanities, says the Teacher, /vanity of
vanities! All is vanity. Ecclesiastes 1:2*

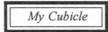

My Cubicle

In my cubicle at work, I have a Xerox copy of my hand and my daughter's hand, side by side.

I have two drawings by my son of Michael Jordan dunking the ball and another of the Bulls on the court against the Celtics, with the Bulls leading 10 to 8.

There are my son's old drawings of Teenage Mutant Ninja Turtles (he'd never draw them now) and my daughter's rendering of an Indian village on a piece of brown paper, crumpled up and smoothed out again to resemble a buffalo skin.

There are school photos of my kids and a couple of shots of the whole family together. There's a picture of my wife looking directly into the camera, and one of my son, just three and a half, at Halloween, wearing a fireman's hat and carrying a hammer and a lunch box, while his sister, about six months old, sits, bundled to immobility, in her stroller with her pacifier in her mouth.

There is also a clear-plastic sandwich bag, holding the now-dried remains of a couple of bright yellow dandelions that my daughter brought on a surprise visit to my cubicle two or three years ago.

----

*The steadfast love of the L*ORD *is from everlasting to everlasting /on those who fear him, /and his righteousness to children's children. Psalm 103:17*

Left Behind

She feels left behind.

He's got a great job. He gets things done around the house. He comes and goes. He talks on the phone. He smiles. He says, "Hi." But he doesn't have time for her. He's busy.

She feels left behind.

She gets the kids up in the morning and prepares them for bed, then sits waiting for him to come home from yet another meeting.

She feels left behind.

Husbands should love their wives as they do their own bodies. He who loves his wife loves himself. For no one ever hates his own body, but he nourishes and tenderly cares for it.
Ephesians 5:28-29

Bliss

"Follow your bliss."

Those words of Joseph Campbell, heard in passing while channel-hopping one night, have stuck with me.

Try to be happy. Strive for those things that make you joyful. Do things that make you feel good.

Not a bad motto for a life, or a faith.

Not a bad inheritance to pass on.

Blessed be the God and Father of our Lord Jesus Christ! By his great mercy he has given us a new birth into a living hope through the resurrection of Jesus Christ from the dead, and into an inheritance that is imperishable, undefiled, and unfading, kept in heaven for you, who are being protected by the power of God through faith for a salvation ready to be revealed in the last time. 1 Peter 1:3-5

Titles II

Down to the end of his days, he will treasure his main title: Daddy.

Let those little children grow, let them become sophisticated adults, let them have their own lives, let them have their own children.

He will always be their Daddy.

Such a mundane word, so rich in meaning.

_____

*When we cry, "Abba! Father!" it is that very
spirit bearing witness with our spirit that we
are children of God. Romans 8:15-16*

Sir

You're older than every single major league baseball player.

You're older than your mother was when she had her last baby.

You're older than the President of the United States.

You've got children already thinking about careers.

You're as old as your father was when he became a grandfather.

So it shouldn't surprise you when someone calls you "sir."

———————————————

Surely you know, for you were born then, /and the number of your days is great! Job 38:21

Wildflower

Look. Here. In the heart of the city, in the alley behind your house, along the edge of your garage, a wildflower blooms.

It is more than two feet tall, and much of its length is covered by thin, fuzzy, light-green leaves.

At the top of the plant are small, light-green pods, perhaps 40 or 50 of them, clustered together like corn on an ear. Two of the pods, their time having arrived, have exploded, like popcorn, into blossom.

This wildflower is called mullein. Each of its blossoms is a delicate yellow. Each has five petals that trumpet out in sharp contrast to the tight constraint of the other, still-germinating pods.

You show your children, and, predictably, your son wants to whack it with a stick. You stop him and explain why it's important to respect living and growing things.

Two weeks later, the wildflower is still there. Still unwhacked.

They are planted in the house of the Lord; /they flourish in the courts of our God. Psalm 92:13

Eating Spurt

My son, for his bedtime snack, has had a leftover piece of pizza, then some barbecue potato chips and is now grazing the kitchen for something else to eat.

"Forget it," I say. "Get to bed."

"But, Dad!" he responds. "I'm real hungry. I'm going through an eating spurt."

You shall eat in plenty and be satisfied, /and praise the name of the LORD your God, /who has dealt wondrously with you. Joel 2:26

> *What He Loves*

We are clustered around the TV together, the whole family, watching "Beauty and the Beast," yet again.

I lie on the floor, half dozing. My son lies down next to me.

"This is what I love," he says. "The whole family, just hanging out together."

Me, too.

Little children, let us love, not in word or speech, but in truth and action. 1 John 3:18

Past the Due Date

Everyone asks about his wife. How's she doing? Is she going stir crazy, stuck at home, waiting? Does she wish she'd stayed at work for a few more weeks? Is she getting any sleep? Isn't it hard for her? Is there any help she needs?

No one asks about him.

Nobody asks how he's doing. Nobody wants to know about the tension that's got him wound tight. Nobody wants to hear about how helpless he feels.

He's feeling sorry for himself. But, hell, it's his pregnancy, too.

Consider my affliction and my trouble. Psalm 25:18

So Much for Plans

It's all planned.

We'll have a picnic in the backyard. We'll barbecue some burgers, have chips and salads and tall, cold drinks.

We'll clean up real quick and then sit around the table together, just the four of us.

And so it goes. The kids are helpful in every way they can think of. The meal goes well. The cleaning up goes smoothly.

We're ready for our time to revel in being a family.

And the phone rings.

With all wisdom and insight he has made known to us the mystery of his will, according to his good pleasure that he set forth in Christ, as a plan for the fullness of time, to gather up all things in him. Things in heaven and things on earth. Ephesians 1:8-10

The Meaning of Fatherhood: Part 4

The secret is:

Fatherhood is more fun than watching sports. More fun than making money. More fun than sex. More fun than driving fast. More fun than drinking hard. More fun than sky-diving. More fun than motorcycles. More fun than rodeos. More fun than gambling. More fun than games. More fun than winning.

Those who are unspiritual do not receive the gifts of God's Spirit, for they are foolishness to them, and they are unable to understand them because they are spiritually discerned.
1 Corinthians 2:14

His Grandfather

It was Independence Day, 1943, when his grandfather died. His father, away in the army, took trains across the country to get back just in time for the funeral.

He was born six years later and given the grandfather's name.

A half century later, he realizes what an honor that was.

The good leave an inheritance to their children's children. Proverbs 13:22

My Kids

Do you want to know about my kids?

All you need to do is

View them together.

It's amazing how much they

Dote on each other (most of the time).

Sometimes, of course, they

Argue. But they are best friends,

Relishing each other's company

And, trading looks and giggles,

Happy to be growing up together.

---

*Now I appeal to you, brothers and sisters, by
the name of our Lord Jesus Christ, that all of
you be in agreement and that there be no
divisions among you, but that you be united in
the same mind and the same purpose.*
1 Corinthians 1:10

A Peaceful Sound

In an especially busy time, I am in my office at home before dawn, working while my wife and kids still sleep.

I feel the house—quiet, peaceful—as I shuffle through a stack of papers.

As I pack my briefcase to leave for a breakfast meeting, I hear the soft footsteps of my still half-asleep son walking to the bathroom.

It is a peaceful sound.

The path of the righteous is like the light of dawn, /which shines brighter and brighter until full day. Proverbs 4:18

Homecoming

He walks up the stairs into the rooms where his children sleep.

He thinks about waking them, but decides against it.

There will be time enough in the morning to tell them that their mother is gone again. This time, she says, she is not coming back.

He is numb with the collision of hundreds of feelings. He feels angry, sad, afraid, alone, empty, rageful, bitter, betrayed, depressed, upset, anxious, abandoned.

"Daddy!" his four-year-old cries out in his sleep.

"I will not leave you orphaned; I am coming to you." John 14:18

The Tall Son

There once was a son from Mt. Kite

Who grew six feet seven in height.

His father was awed.

The boy's shoulders were broad.

And he'd hug him with all of his might.

He had a son whose name was Saul, a handsome young man. There was not a man among the people of Israel more handsome than he; he stood head and shoulders above everyone else.
1 Samuel 9:2

Double Jeopardy

It would have been one thing if the two boys, covered with mud, had stood at the back door and called for help.

But, no, they walked through the house, getting mud all over the floors and rugs and walls.

Their father was never so angry.

He stripped their clothes off them and spanked them before putting them in the bathtub together.

After washing, they got in their pajamas and were sent right to bed without supper.

It was then that the washer broke because of the thick mud embedded in their clothes.

Their father came in their room and spanked them all over again.

You must understand this, my beloved; let everyone be quick to listen, slow to speak, slow to anger; for your anger does not produce God's righteousness. James 1:19

Nine

My son turns nine tomorrow. I can't believe how quickly those years have gone.

In another nine years, he'll be 18 and away at college.

In another nine years, he'll be 27 and starting on a career and maybe even married.

In another nine years, he'll be 36 and probably a father himself.

In another nine years . . . he'll be my age.

So Jacob served seven years for Rachel, and they seemed to him but a few days because of the love he had for her. Genesis 29:20

Thoughts

He always wondered why his father left. His mother never talked about it, and he was too young—or too innocent—to remember what led up to it.

He thought:

Did my father plan this, setting aside money, studying options, and all the time smiling a false smile?

Or did my father run away on the spur of the moment, in a fit of shame or despair or lust?

Or was my father lured away?

Or driven away?

Did my mother push him out? Did I irritate him too much? (I was only a kid.)

Did he leave even though he loved me?

Or did he leave because he didn't love me?

Why do you hide your face? /Why do you forget our affliction and oppression? Psalm 44:24

Fathering

Fathering isn't a game. You don't win or lose. It's not play. There are no rules.

It's not like sports. It's not like work. There are no stats. There are no commissions. Your family doesn't have a father of the month. You're it for better or worse, month in and month out.

There are no touchdown runs in fathering. No end zone dances. No slam dunks. No five-hit shut-outs.

No retirement, either.

So I do not run aimlessly, nor do I box as
though beating the air; but I punish my body
and enslave it, so that after proclaiming to
others I myself should not be disqualified.
1 Corinthians 9:26-27

> *Regarding Sex*

You have to understand, children, that there is another level of communication that has nothing to do with words. It is a way of talking and laughing and grieving and rejoicing and arguing and whispering and shouting and chattering and playing that involves touch and gesture. It's another way to give and receive, to speak and hear. It is deeper than words. It is as profound as music—and as mysterious as life.

Come, my beloved, /let us go forth into the fields, /and lodge in the villages; /let us go out early to the vineyards, /and see whether the vines have budded, /whether the grape blossoms have opened /and the pomegranates are in bloom. /There I will give you my love. Song of Songs 7:11-12

> Seasons

"What's your favorite season?" my six-year-old daughter asks.

"Winter," I say.

"Because you like to shovel the snow," she tells me.

"Yes, and I like to look at the snow."

My nine-year-old son says, "I like summer and winter."

My daughter replies, "I like spring, summer and winter . . . And fall!"

Now that I think about it, so do I.

For everything there is a season, and a time for every matter under heaven. Ecclesiastes 3:1

The Meeting

As you're going into the important meeting, you get the message that your son is in the principal's office, ill.

You call your wife's office. No answer.

You call one neighbor. Then, a second. Finally a third one is home and can go over to the school and get the boy until the regular babysitter arrives and takes him home.

You explain to your groggy son about the arrangement. He doesn't respond. He just wants to get off the phone.

You enter your meeting.

———————————

Just as you do not know how the breath comes to the bones in the mother's womb, so you do not know the work of God. Ecclesiastes 11:15

Super Dad: One

You know how fallible you are. Remember the errors in the report you turned in at the office?

You know how lazy you can be. Remember the list of chores your wife gave you? (Now, where is that piece of paper?)

You know how bull-headed you can be. Remember how you got lost on the way to your mother's—your mother's!—house and wouldn't ask for directions?

But, to your kids, you know all, see all and understand everything.

To them, you are Super Dad.

"Be perfect, therefore, as your heavenly Father is perfect." Matthew 5:48

A Father's Primer

Here's how it's going to be:

(1) On Christmas Day you will be awakened by your children at six A.M. and expected to be intensely interested in the gifts that Santa has brought them. Later in the day, you might be able to nap—if you're lucky.

(2) When you go for walks with you children, you will be expected to carry them from time to time—although to you it will seem that they only walk from time to time. You will find that there is nothing quite so rewarding as carrying your child. Or so tiring.

(3) You will have to change your child's dirty diapers until the child agrees to go through potty training. You will be expected to cheer your child's efforts at potty training, and such cheering, you may rest assured, will not be insincere.

"Did I conceive all these people? Did I give birth to them, that you should say to me, 'Carry them in your bosom, as a nurse carries a sucking child?'" Numbers 11:12

Great Grandpa

He can't remember much of the hard times. He can't remember much of the good times, either.

He lives with a flow of images and feelings from the past, unconnected usually, like waking dreams.

He doesn't know these faces around him. There is some celebration. He doesn't know why.

The little children are cute. And they kiss him so softly.

So even to old age and gray hairs, /O God, do not forsake me, /until I proclaim your might /to all the generations to come. Psalm 71:18

His World

His father moved through life as if he was a slave.

It wasn't that he had chains on his wrists and ankles, but he might as well have, the way he bowed and scraped to everyone.

His was a world of tight spaces and deep fears.

His son saw that world, and came to despise it.

I want you to be free from anxieties.
1 Corinthians 7:32

> ## Good Enough

He's a good enough father, isn't he? He puts food on the table. He helps the kids with their homework. He loves their mother. He loves them.

He even baked cookies one Christmas. But is he good enough?

He's not very gregarious. He doesn't like the kids' friends. He doesn't like how his kids spend their money. Sometimes—maybe a lot of times—he doesn't exactly like his kids. So is he good enough?

Sure, he is. He's better than the guy next door. He's better than not having a father at all. He's good enough. He's sure he is.

Isn't he?

Do not, therefore, abandon that confidence of yours; it brings a great reward. Hebrews 10:35

Lover

She writes the grocery lists for him. She takes the kids to the doctor. She runs to the post office and the drug store and the hardware store and the library and the church bazaar and Radio Shack. She gets supper ready and cleans the bathroom. She fixes breakfast for the kids and a lunch for him to take to work. She tells him when his tie doesn't match. She takes his messages.

She's his wife.

She's also his lover.

"This at last is bone of my bones /and flesh of my flesh; /this one shall be called Woman."
Genesis 2:23

The Lurch

He answers the phone and feels a lurch as if the floor has fallen out from under him.

His daughter's in trouble again, out past curfew, drinking, who knows what else.

He sets the phone down and pulls on his clothes.

She was always such a sweet little girl, he tells himself.

He just doesn't know her anymore.

The word of the Lord came to me: Mortal, you are living in the midst of a rebellious house, who have eyes to see but do not see, who have ears to hear but do not hear. Ezekiel 12:1-2

Out the Door

I love my kids, but this morning, after being cooped up with them for two days, I'm eager to get away.

I want to go to a coffee shop, or a bookstore, or the library, or the store. Anyplace!

I just want to get away from my sick son and his "Dad, I'm bored" sister.

My wife is off today and can pick up the slack.

I'm out the door. (Back at three.)

The Lord has anointed me; /he has sent me to bring good news to the oppressed, /to bind up the broken hearted, /to proclaim liberty to the captives, /and release to the prisoners. Isaiah 61:1

Forgotten

His grave isn't marked, and neither are the graves of his children, scattered around the city in other cemeteries.

His grandchildren, the older ones, have some memory of him: gruff, formal, distant. But they rarely bring that memory to mind.

Some of his great-grandchildren have seen a few photos of him on those rare occasions when the photo album is pulled out and looked at. The others have never even seen a picture of him or know his name.

His great-great-grandchildren are babies now. They crawl as he crawled when he was an infant; they notice, as he first noticed, the sunlight streaming in the window onto the floor; their blood—his blood—flows and fuels and feeds.

They don't know and probably never will know that he worked for the railroad, and drank too much, and was tongue-tied in the presence of children.

———————————————

For the LORD is good; /his steadfast love endures forever, /and his faithfulness to all generations. Psalm 100:5

> *Work and Family*

You want to make money, sure. It's good to be able to make life comfortable for your wife and kids—and yourself.

You want to enjoy your work, too. It's good to have a job that's challenging and fulfilling.

But you engage in a quiet guerilla campaign against your bosses and yourself to keep your work within reasonable limits, to keep your work in its place.

Too much time spent at work, and you won't hear your son's question as you doze off during the football game.

Too much of your life spent at work, and you'll look back and wonder why.

Instead of bronze I will bring gold, /instead of iron I will bring silver; /instead of wood, bronze, /instead of stones, iron. /I will appoint Peace as your overseer /and Righteousness as your task master. Isaiah 60:17

Tom's Dad

The phone rings at eight on a weekend morning. It's my son's friend. I tell him everyone's asleep.

As I doze off again, I remember how I would roam the neighborhood in the hours after dawn, waiting for it to be late enough to call for my friend at his back door.

"Yoooooooo, Tom!"

Tom's father was usually still asleep, too.

Do not forsake your friend or the friend of your parent. Proverbs 27:10

Fireflies

As dusk descends, the children run screaming with laughter across the front lawns.

Suddenly, your son stops, leaps awkwardly into the air and comes down with his small hand clenched into a fist.

Inside the tiny fist is his treasure—a firefly.

"We catched (sic) some and let them go," he tells you. "We hold them in our hands. A lot of times they tickle. They blink. They're soft. And cold."

He turns, reaches quickly to snare another firefly and then lets it go.

Sort of like what a father does with his children.

Here I am in your hands. Do with me as seems good and right to you. Jeremiah 26:14

As It Should Be

I'm pruning dead branches from the crabapple tree in the backyard.

I saw through the thick limbs with a curved saw at the end of a pole.

It's tiring work, and the muscles of my arm are soon aching.

My six-year-old daughter stands nearby, watching. She wants to help, and, every once in a while, I have her clip small branches from the main one.

Soon, however, she says she's going out in front to play with her brother.

That's as it should be. As crabapple trees are meant to be pruned, children are meant to play.

I will not be a burden, because I do not want what is yours but you; for children ought not to lay up for their parents, but parents for their children. 2 Corinthians 12:14

$$\boxed{\textit{Break}}$$

He put the boy in his car right away and drove the three miles to the hospital quickly.

The boy cried and moaned in the back seat, and screamed as his father picked him up to carry him into the emergency room.

The nurse looked at the broken arm and filled out a form.

The doctor came and went.

An hour later, the boy wore a bright white cast.

It was only then that the father's hands began to shake.

Blessed be the God and Father of our Lord Jesus Christ, the Father of mercies and the God of all consolation, who consoles us in all our affliction, so that we may be able to console those who are in any affliction with the consolation with which we ourselves are consoled by God. 2 Corinthians 1:3-4

She is Sweet

She is something of a lost soul, but she is sweet.

She has had a hard time with life. But she tries and tries.

She's just not good at a lot of it. Money runs through her hands. She's been unlucky at love.

But she loves you. And you love her.

Your wife worries so much about her.

You worry, too. You are sad for her. But, when your daughter comes home for yet another stay, you can't help but be happy to see her again.

Be content with what you have; for he has said,
"I will never leave you or forsake you."
Hebrews 13:5

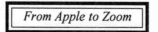

From Apple to Zoom

In the office, on the weekend, I take care of some loose ends while my six-year-old daughter types at the computer.

She has decided to type out three words for each letter of the alphabet.

"How do you spell 'apple'?" she asks

I tell her.

"What other words begin with 'a'?"

"How about 'arm' and 'all'?"

"How do you spell them?"

I tell her.

And so it goes for an hour—me doing my busy work, her asking the spellings and making her way through the alphabet.

We end with zoo, zebra and zoom.

———————————————

A word fitly spoken /is like apples of gold in a setting of silver. Proverbs 25:11

A Bonus (Sort Of)

He's marrying the love of his life. And, as an extra bonus (sort of), he's becoming stepfather to her two teenage daughters.

Not only is he having to live through all the changes that happen when you turn from bachelor to husband, when you move from the easy choices of an individual to the negotiated decisions of a couple.

He's also having to accept the new responsibility of being father to two young people he's still getting to know. And these two girls still aren't all that sure what they think of the new arrangement.

Marriage is complicated enough without the complexities of immediate fatherhood as well.

I will instruct you and teach you the way you should go; /I will counsel you with my eye upon you. Psalm 32:8

Waiting

At the pizzeria, we place our order. "Twenty minutes," the man says.

My daughter and I go for a walk down the street, past the stores and doorways and other restaurants, to kill time.

In the distance, dark clouds loom over downtown. But here, the sky is clear and the setting sun lights up the full green of the leaves on trees lining the curb.

The contrast is a beauty to remember for the rest of our lives.

My daughter's antsy to go back to see if the pizza's ready yet.

The heavens are telling the glory of God; /and the firmament proclaims his handiwork. Psalm 19:1

The Knife

My nine-year-old son talked his mother into letting him buy a pocketknife.

It's a cheap thing, but it has the full set of blades, corkscrew, tiny scissors, bottle opener and what not.

He's so proud of his knife. It has an edge of danger and the feel of a real, adult tool. It's another step in his becoming a man.

Part of me wants to keep it from him. I worry about him hurting himself or someone else.

The better part of me knows I have to risk that.

———————————————

Train children in the right way, /and when they are old, they will not stray. Proverbs 22:6

Worries and Laughter

You stand in the doorway of your son's room.

He's in deep sleep.

A teenager now, he fills the bed, no longer the tiny baby whose breathing you so closely monitored.

You were always afraid then that, without any warning, he'd just stop breathing.

You would stand there, straining your eyes to see the slight movement of his chest that showed he was still inhaling and exhaling.

Now those worries seem so long ago, so silly in a way. You miss that little baby.

In his sleep, your son laughs.

"Whoever welcomes one such child in my name welcomes me." Matthew 18:5

| *Colleague* |

The father trims the wood to fit, and looks through the frame of the new house-to-be to see his son hammering at the other corner.

The boy—he's a man now, really—is deeply tanned. He has his shirt off. He wears a bandana around his head to keep the sweat out of his eyes.

The father is filled with joy that his son has chosen—for now, at least—to work at his side.

As for Titus, he is my partner and co-worker in your service. 2 Corinthians 8:23

The Argument

During the argument, the children worry that the parents will get a divorce.

"It's not like that," the father tells the children later. "Moms and Dads have to fight sometimes to express their feelings, to get each other's attention, to release tensions."

He says, "I know it's hard on you. It's hard on us. But we have to go through this. It's important that we're honest with each other—about what we think and, more important, about what we feel."

That's what he tells the children.

This is the part he doesn't tell them: "I loved the woman who is your mother before you were born, and I will love her after you have moved away. We are in a dance. It will last a lifetime. And beyond. We hug tight to each other. If sometimes that hug looks like a wrestling match, so be it. It's all part of the same dance."

What the children don't say to him but think when the argument is over and the parents are smiling again at each other: "This thing called love is a power."

When I enter my house I shall find rest with her; /for companionship with her has no bitterness, /and life with her has no pain, but gladness and joy. Wisdom 8:16

Super Dad: Two

Your son comes running in to announce, "There's a bat under the back porch!"

This, you realize immediately, is a job for Super Dad. You leap out of your chair and run down the stairs to find your kids and a handful of neighbor kids crowding around the obviously injured bat lying still on the cement.

You shoo the kids back and look at the bat. It is brown and leathery-looking. And ugly. It has large ears and a mouthful of teeth.

You start to move stuff away from the bat, and suddenly it begins flopping around on the cement and making a dry clicking sound.

You almost jump out of your skin. And the kids all laugh at you.

But you see it's no laughing matter. The bat's right wing is completely missing.

I will break your proud glory. Leviticus 26:19

Super Dad: Three

You've got to do something. There's a bat under your back porch, alive, dangerous and fatally injured. One of its wings is missing.

You know what you have to do, but you don't want to do it. You've got to put the bat out of its misery.

There is a shovel near at hand. But slamming the bat over the head with the flat blade of the shovel is too violent for your taste. You really would have preferred to have an act of God, perhaps a bolt of lightning, take care of this. But there's not a cloud in the sky.

Then, nearby, you see a 20-pound cinder-block brick.

The end comes in an instant for the bat. It isn't hurting anymore. You use the shovel to pick up the limp body and slide it into a plastic bag that you then drop in a garbage can.

The kids watch in silent awe. But you don't feel like Super Dad.

Death has come up into our windows. Jeremiah 9:21

August 9

> *Guessing Game*

My daughter moans with an ear ache. It's seven A.M. She's been up for an hour. We can't get to the doctor's office until nine at the earliest and probably not until later.

It's been only two hours since she had a dose of Tylenol, but I say, "Let's give her some more anyway."

It works. She goes back to sleep.

I'm glad. I had no second plan.

Is there no balm in Gilead? /Is there no physician there? Jeremiah 8:22

Old Ways

He doesn't understand. It wasn't like this back home. Here, in this new country, things are different. The kids don't follow the old ways. They don't want to hear the old stories.

What else can he give them?

———————————————————

And now, my children, listen to me: /happy are those who keep my ways. Proverbs 8:32

Sun and Son

In the quiet, a month or so after the birth, the poet was filled with joy and pride at his newborn son and sat down to write a song of happiness.

But this is what he wrote:

As the sun sets,

I watch my son

and envy him

his future.

"Are you jealous for my sake? Would that all the LORD's people were prophets, and that the LORD would put his spirit in them." Numbers 11:29

I am a touchstone for my children, like the base in a game of tag.

As long as they have me within reach, they feel totally safe.

When they feel adventurous, they start to roam. But when things get scary, it's back to base they go.

Each time, though, they roam farther and farther.

———————————————

Trust in the LORD forever, /for in the LORD GOD /you have an everlasting rock. Isaiah 26:4

Painting

He paints his son's bedroom.

He paints over the Spackled holes. He paints over the pencil scribblings. He paints over where the colorful wall-paper border of stuffed animals used to be, and over the dirt spot on the ceiling where his son once threw a dirty rubber ball.

The room looks so pristine when he's done.

It's not his son's room any more. But now the father can finally allow himself to grieve over the boy's death.

The King was deeply moved and went up to the chamber over the gate, and wept,; and as he went, he said, "O my son Absolom, my son, my son Absolom! Would I had died instead of you." 2 Samuel 18:33

Veteran

He's been farmed out to one of the branch offices. He knows what this means.

Once, when he was young, he would sneer at the old ones who'd settled into a rut, willing to just get by.

Now, he's one of the old ones. He's coasting.

Was he wrong before? Is he wrong now?

What will his kids think?

_____

If you gathered nothing in your youth, /how can you find anything in your old age? /How attractive is sound judgment in the gray-haired, /and for the aged to possess good counsel! Sirach 25:3-4

Cop

You don't like it that your son's a cop.

He comes over on a Sunday morning, fresh from the overnight shift, and sits with you at the kitchen table, eating waffles and telling you stories.

You know enough to know that his stories are carefully selected. There are details he leaves out because they'd get you concerned. There are stories he never tells.

You don't like the gun he wears in the holster at his hip.

Do not envy the violent /and do not choose any of their ways; /for the perverse are an abomination to the Lord, /but the upright are in his confidence. Proverbs 3:31-32

Frog Heaven

The frog dies.

You take the body out of the fish tank and put it in a plastic bag and carry it out to the backyard.

Your son stays inside. He doesn't want to watch.

Your daughter comes with you.

You dig a hole in the dirt under the tree, put the bag containing the frog's body in the hole, and cover it over with dirt.

You tell your daughter, and later your son, that Froggy is in frog heaven.

You hope there is such a place.

The righteous know the needs of their animals.
Proverbs 12:10

August 17

Vacation: Day One

In the cab on the way to the airport, my children are excited and nervous. They're about to take their first flight.

I am nervous, too, although I've flown often enough.

I have this horrible image of the plane going down and killing all of us. And the worst of it is that, in the final moments before impact, I would have to watch my children, still so new and fresh to life, realize that they were about to die.

It's an irrational fear, of course. My kids, my wife and I will be safer in the plane than on the highway.

But later, as the plan taxis to the runway, my stomach starts clutching convulsively.

And moments after take-off, even before the "Fasten Seatbelt" sign is turned off, I have to hurry down the aisle to the plane's bathroom, where I am violently ill.

O Lord, my heart is not lifted up, /my eyes are not raised too high. Psalm 131:1

Vacation: Day Two

In the mountains, under a hazy sky, we walk along the shore of a small lake. The bright, solid colors of our shirts—reds, yellows, blues—form a beautiful counterpoint to the tree green and rock tan of the landscape around us.

My nine-year-old son seems to grow in maturity before my eyes as he devours each new experience of our trip. He leads our hike. He follows a chipmunk to its hole. He spots three moose while exploring a side path.

His six-year-old sister, though, is overwhelmed by all the newness. She is touchy, quick to anger, quick to tears. She stays close by, needing attention and reassurance.

My wife and I cradle her closely, even as we fill with wonder at her brother's growing independence.

If any of you is lacking in wisdom, ask God, who gives to all generously and ungrudgingly, and it will be given to you. James 1:5

> *Vacation: Day Three*

A nagging thought: I've forgotten to leave my bosses a phone number where they can reach me while I'm away.

I realized my oversight the first day out, but we still hadn't gotten settled into our cabin, so I put it off.

Yesterday, I was enjoying the cabin and the mountains too much. Who, I asked myself, could think of work at a time like this? So I didn't call.

This morning, finally, I call.

Everything is fine. No one needs to talk to me. No emergencies need to be taken care of.

I don't leave my number.

"Blessed be the Lord, who has given rest to his people Israel according to all that he promised; not one word has failed of all his good promise." 1 Kings 8:56

Vacation: Day Four

The four of us have climbed mountain trails, watched hummingbirds feed on nectar and sat together around the fireplace. We've eaten all our meals together (what an unusual treat) and witnessed a huge rainbow over the neighboring ridge. We've sung songs, gone shopping, played cards. We've had quiet mornings and cozy evenings. We heard lectures on mountainmen, water-coloring and beavers. We've seen storms march with majestic pace across the floor of the valley below. We've been together as a family as we never have before.

We declare to you what we have seen and heard so that you also may have fellowship with us; and truly our fellowship is with the Father and with his Son Jesus Christ. We are writing these things so that our joy may be complete. 1 John 1:3-4

> *Vacation: Day Five*

My daughter walks along the forest path in front of me, swinging her arms in an unconscious gesture of well-being. Her bearing is regal. Her back is straight. She is tall. She is very much herself.

"You have made known to me the ways of life; /you will make me full of gladness with your presence. Acts 2:28

Vacation: Day Six

In the last moments of dusk, my son and I trudge along the stream with the rest of the hiking group. We are a few steps from the beaver pond, and our guide has alerted us to keep silent.

We tip-toe—some in thick boots, some in soft running shoes—along the slope around the pond. The darkness is now nearly full, and we lean forward in hopes of catching sight of one of the beavers.

"Kerplunk!"

It sounds like a large rock dropped into the water but it's really a signal from one diving beaver to the others that something threatening is nearby.

We hear four kerplunks in all during the 45 minutes we stand there in the dark, leaning forward, silent except for occasional quick whispers. We hear one beaver gnawing on a tree, but can't see him.

In the dimness, I watch my son crouch—quiet, attentive, alert. His eyes are wide and watching. His ears are open and listening.

As we walk back to camp, he is up near the front of the line, carrying his own flashlight, finding his own way.

"Stop and consider the wondrous works of God." Job 37:14

Vacation: Day Seven

The mountains around our cabin, so looming, so huge, are never still.

Their face is always changing as the sun rises, passes over them and sets. One peak is awash in sunlight while another is covered in shadow from a passing cloud. The angle of the light makes one stand of timber look like a lawn of trees. Another seems like a carpet. In still another, I can make out each tree in all its individuality.

After dark, even the silhouettes of the ridges change, as the stars come out, as the clouds shift, as the moon makes its own transit across the sky.

In the half-light just before dawn, the trees, the shrubs, the flowers, the rocks and the other cabins are all shades of grey, awaiting the enlivening light of dawn.

Great is the Lord and greatly to be praised /in the city of our God. /His holy mountain, beautiful in elevation, /is the joy of all the earth. Psalm 48:1

Vacation: Day Eight

We pack our suitcases, eat breakfast, clean the cabin, check out, stop in town for souvenirs, drive three hours along the scenic route to the airport, check our bags, have a snack, get on the plane, go through take-off, sit through the two-hour flight, go through landing, get off the plane, walk through the terminal, find the baggage claim area, grab our bags, flag a cab, ride for an hour through surprisingly thick evening traffic, arrive at our house, climb up the stairs, unlock the door and start opening windows to fill the place with fresh air.

And I remember I forgot to worry about the plane crashing.

"Are not two sparrows sold for a penny? Yet not one of them will fall to the ground apart from your Father. And even the hairs of your head are all counted. So do not be afraid; you are of more value than many sparrows."
Matthew 10:29-31

Resemblances

The waiter reminds you of your youngest son at college.

In the young saleswoman, you see your daughter, just starting at that law firm on the East Coast.

You think of your oldest as you work with the rising hot-shot at the office.

It's small consolation for not being able to tuck them in at night any more.

"Come, let us look one another in the face."
2 Chronicles 25:17

A Spanking

I will never forget the moment when my two-year-old daughter grabbed the extra-sharp kitchen knife from the open dishwasher and ran giggling all the way to the front room where she leaped on the couch, playfully evading me as I ran full speed after her.

I will always know how close I came to tragedy then.

It was the only time I spanked her.

Hear, my child, and accept my words, /that the years of your life may be many. Proverbs 4:10

Way Too Fast

It's not that he's old or conservative or stodgy.

But he has this look about his eyes as if everything were going too fast, way too fast. His wife is aging—gracefully, to be sure, but aging nonetheless. His teenage daughter is growing into an assured young woman. His baby son is a baby no longer, entering first grade and taking lessons in *tae kwon do*.

He sinks deeper into his Lay-Z-Boy.

---

*"Therefore every scribe who has been trained
for the kingdom of heaven is like the master of
a household who brings out of his treasure
what is new and what is old." Matthew 13:52*

Fireworks

At the ballpark: fireworks after the game. The rockets and the bursts are breath-taking. The booms of the explosions are awesome. Young couples hug each other closer, their eyes trained on the sky, their mouths open in wonder. Teenagers giggle and poke each other and cheer each new pyrotechnic extravaganza.

Our kids, though, are frightened. It's too bright, too loud, too close. We get up to leave, and shepherd them down the stairs and out of the stadium.

They trust us to protect them.

We do.

For he will command his angels concerning you /to guard you in all your ways. /On their hands they will bear you up, /so that you will not dash your foot against a stone. Psalm 91:11-12

> ### Voicemail IV

"Hi, dear. It's me.

"The guy is coming over this afternoon to give an estimate for painting the back porch. We agreed to go with him if the cost is reasonable, right?

"Also, I wanted to remind you that I'm going out with Joy tonight for coffee. But I won't leave until nine o'clock so I can help put the kids to bed.

"That package you were expecting didn't come today. And remind me to tell you about what your son did when I dropped him off at school today.

"Oh, and your mother called.

"Gotta go! Bye! I love you!"

O my dove, in the clefts of the rock, /in the covert of the cliff, /let me see your face, /let me hear your voice; /for your voice is sweet, /and your face is lovely. Song of Songs 2:14

Shepherd

You think of the good shepherd and you imagine your own father.

He's got the lost lamb across his broad shoulders, and he's heading back to the flock.

He's there, silent and steady, with his flock—day-in, day-out, through the night, through the seasons.

He knows his lambs. And they know him.

———————————————

I am the good shepherd. I know my own and my own know me, just as the Father knows me and I know the Father. John 10:14-15

The Thing to Remember

The think to remember is that we can't bottle our children for future study. The only time to enjoy who they are now is now. Never again will my son's shoulders look exactly that way as he skips through the house to his room. Never again will my daughter have that particular look of delight as she holds a baby duck in her hands. There are riches to come in the future, but these treasures will evaporate tomorrow like the dew.

"Do not store up for yourselves treasures on earth, where moth and rust consume and where thieves break in and steal; but store up for yourselves treasures in heaven, where neither moth nor rust consumes and where thieves do not break in and steal. For where your treasure is, there your heart will be also." Matthew 6:19-21

"Get In"

He is walking in the pouring rain, coming home after working late at the store where he bags groceries.

It had been such a bright, clear day. Now, the cold rain pelts his hair and clothes. His shoes are soaked, and so is he.

He shivers as he stands at the corner, waiting for the light to change.

A car pulls up. "Get in," his dad says.

He jumps into the warmth within.

If a brother or sister is naked and lacks daily food, and one of you says to them, "Go in peace; keep warm and eat your fill," and yet you do not supply their bodily needs, what is the good of that? James 2:15-16

Question and Answer

"Dad, is 52, take away 16, 44?"

"No, it's 36."

Silence.

"You're right."

"Make known to them the way they are to go and the things they are to do." Exodus 18:20

Going To Be A Father

He's 17, and he knows he should be worried. He's new at his job and still newly married. And now his wife's expecting a baby.

He knows this is going to mean hard times. He and his wife are hardly making ends meet now. They're hardly adults themselves.

How will they pay for everything a baby needs? For formula and diapers and clothes and a crib and a car seat and rattles?

He knows he should be worried. Instead, he's walking on air.

He's going to be a father. Can you top that?

Like arrows in the hand of a warrior /are the sons of one's youth. /Happy is the man who has /his quiver full of them. Psalm 127:4-5

| Tears |

You see your wife cry at *The Lion King*, and you're jealous.

You see your children cry, too.

Crying is something you should be able to do. It's so natural. So cathartic.

Yet so foreign to you.

A time to weep, and a time to laugh; /a time to mourn, and a time to dance. Ecclesiastes 3:4

First Day of School

We bring our son and daughter to the first day of school.

Oh, I would like to be in their place.

———————————

Rid yourselves, therefore, of all malice, and all guile, insincerity, envy, and all slander. Like newborn infants, long for the pure, spiritual milk, so that by it you may grow into salvation. 1 Peter 2:1-2

| Television |

How much of my interest in history came from watching Davy Crockett on TV when I was a boy?

How much of my son's interest in art springs from watching the Teenage Mutant Ninja Turtles—Michelangelo, Leonardo, Raphael and Donatello—on the tube?

Will my daughter become a lawyer or doctor after watching re-runs of the Bill Cosby Show?

Television can be a window on a vast world—as well as on a vast wasteland.

A time to seek, and a time to lose; /a time to keep, and a time to throw away. Ecclesiastes 3:6

> Been There

When he was young, his bosses were like gods.

They acted that way, and he saw them that way.
They handed down orders and dispensed wisdom. He
listened. And obeyed.

Now, he is older. He's been a boss himself a few
times.

His bosses still act like gods. But he doesn't pay
much attention any more.

He's been there before.

---

*"Are you the firstborn of the human race?
/Were you brought forth before the hills? /Have
you listened in the council of God? /And do you
limit wisdom to yourself?" Job 15:7-8*

Tete-a-tete

You chase your kids out of the living room so you and your wife can talk.

You lock them out of your bedroom so you can be together.

You're deaf to their pleas for attention so you can listen to each other.

You ignore their questions so you can trade tales and chatter at the kitchen table.

The best thing a father can do for his children is to love his wife.

Enjoy life with the wife you love. Ecclesiastes 9:9

Uncle Eddie

When my father was at work, I would sit with my Uncle Eddie and watch the Cubs on TV.

He would pass along books to me when he was finished with them.

He took my brothers and me to special movies— *The Alamo, D-Day, Ben-Hur*. He'd buy us lunch at a diner, and then we'd walk across the street to the theater.

He died when I was at college.

I still regret missing his funeral.

Blessed are those who mourn, for they will be comforted. Matthew 5:4

Manliness

I will never agree that men and women are essentially different.

I will not agree, for example, that women have intuition and men have drive. That women are soft and men are hard. That women nurture and men discipline.

My father sews. My sister is a cop.

I like to cuddle with my kids. Is this not manly?

It is to peace that God has called you. Wife, for all you know, you might save your husband. Husband, for all you know, you might save your wife. 1 Corinthians 7:15-16

Business Trip: First Day

I leave in the mid-afternoon for the four-hour drive. I'll be away for only a couple of days, and the kids are so tied up in their TV show that they hardly say good-bye.

It's a sunny day, and the highway is fairly empty. I fly along listening to music and a tape on the Civil War.

At the hotel, I get settled, order supper and call home.

It's early evening, and things are chaotic. The kids are tired and whiny. My wife is tired and irritated.

I'm tired, too. But when the call is done, I've got a quiet evening to look forward to, and a room service meal on the way. I might even blow off that book I was going to read and watch the basketball game.

My wife still has to get the kids to bed.

I will both lie down and sleep in peace; /for you alone, O Lord, make me lie down in safety.
Psalm 4:8

| Business Trip: Second Day |

After a meeting in one city, I drive two hours to another for three more meetings.

That night, I laze in the hotel's sauna. I luxuriate in the whirlpool. I take some desultory turns around the pool.

Loneliness isn't so bad sometimes.

A time to keep silence, and a time to speak.
Ecclesiastes 3:7

> *Business Trip: Third Day*

The hours drop away as the car pounds down the highway. This is the day my wife works late. This is the day I get the kids at the babysitter's after work. This is the day I get home from my trip, and I want to be on time.

I'm only five minutes late, and the kids are glad to see me.

"What are we having for supper?" they ask.

I'm home.

So there shall be a highway from Assyria /for the remnant that is left of his people, /as there was for Israel /when they came up from the land of Egypt. Isaiah 11:16

$$\boxed{\textit{Missing}}$$

It's been 27 hours now, and he is frantic. The police have looked for his daughter. They're driven up and down the streets and alleys of the neighborhood and have come up empty. He's checked with all of her friends yet one more time. They still have nothing to tell him. His wife is rigid with anxiety. He is so afraid.

Save me, O God, /for the waters have come up to my neck. /I sink in deep mire, /where there is no foothold; /I have come into deep waters, /and the flood sweeps over me. Psalm 69:1-3

Fresh Air

His boss is as big as a house. She's going to have a baby.

There is joy and excitement in this that transcends the mundane details of business profit and loss, the carefully delineated relationship of employer and employee. Who can stop from smiling?

A new life is being born. The evidence is there for all to see.

It's a breath of fresh air in the dusty world of columned numbers and Xeroxed expense accounts.

"My soul magnifies the Lord, /and my spirit rejoices in God my Savior, /for he has looked with favor on the lowliness of his servant. /surely, from now on all generations will call me blessed." Luke 1:46-48

September 16

Sick Son

My son is sick. I skip breakfast. I rearrange my morning. I go in to work early. I'll leave around noon to get home in time to relieve my wife (who has rearranged her day and will go into her work late).

I'm happy to do it.

I'm happy I have a job that lets me do it.

Isaac said to his father Abraham, "Father!" And he said, "Here I am, my son." Genesis 22:7

The Meaning of Fatherhood: Part 5

I don't know how many more miles it is.

I don't know which teacher you'll have next year.

I don't know how much longer you'll have to wait for Mom to get home.

I don't know why boys sweat more than girls.

I don't know whom you're going to marry.

I don't know if your friend has gotten your letter yet.

I don't know if the store will have the toy you want.

I'm sorry. I just don't know.

"Who is this that darkens counsel by words without knowledge? /Gird up your loins like a man, /I will question you, and you shall declare to me." Job 38:2-3

Diet

There once was a father named Daniel

Whose stomach was much more than ample.

He was forced by his clan

To eat no more Spam

Or pizza or eggs by the panful.

---

*"Look at Behemoth, /which I made just as I
made you; it eats grass like an ox." Job 40:15*

Helllllooooooooo???

I'm walking through a food court at the mall, and, as I pass a table of two teenage girls and a boy about the same age, I overhear one of the girls say, "So I said, 'Earth to Mom: Hellllloooooooo??? . . . .'"

Immediately, the image pops in my head of my six-year-old daughter, holding up her hand, leaning her head to one side, bugging out her eyes, and saying in a way all her own, "Earth to Dad: Hellllooooooo???"

You rang?

_____

Remember your creator in the days of your youth. Ecclesiastes 12:1

Cuss Words

His son brings home a note from his teacher. The boy was heard using a cuss word. The teacher is "very disappointed."

The father writes a note back to the teacher: "I've talked to my son. I've told him not to use such language. Thank you for bringing this to my attention."

The father does not add, "He's never heard such words like that around here."

He's not that much of a hypocrite.

From the same mouth came blessing and cursing. My brothers and sisters, this ought not to be so. James 3:10

september_21

| Going to Church |

At first, it's a triumph if you don't have to leave the service more than once each Sunday because of their crying.

Then, you feel good if you can get them to be quiet at least for a few minutes during the prayers.

Later, if they can sit still for the entire ceremony, you are ecstatic.

Much later, if they kneel and stand at the right times, you're pleased as punch.

Finally, you're ready to work with them to understand what's happening at the altar—what the priest does, what the congregation does, what it all means.

You want to help them see the mystery and the faith in the ritual.

But, by then, you've almost lost sight of it yourself.

Let what you heard from the beginning abide in you. If what you heard from the beginning abides in you, then you will abide in the Son and in the Father. And this is what he has promised us, eternal life. 1 John 2:24-25

Son

Sure, I'm not

Objective, but

No other son is sweeter than mine.

Saul said to him, "Whose son are you, young man?" And David answered, "I am the son of your servant Jesse the Bethlehemite." 1 Samuel 17:58

Daughter

Do you know what it's like to

Await the

Unfolding of a blossom,

Glistening with dew,

Heavy with potential,

Tender, yet strong

Enough for what will come

Regardless?

How great a forest is set ablaze by a small fire!
James 3:5

| Memory |

Living in another city, he is unable to visit his father's grave. Instead, he visits his dad in his memory.

He can feel his father standing behind him, so tall, reaching over to pat both his pudgy cheeks in a playful caress.

He can hear his father's voice reading *The Runaway Bunny* for the umpteenth time at his bedside.

He can smell the sweat in his father's clothes as he'd walk through the front door at the end of the work day, looking for a welcome-home hug from his kids.

He can see the way his father walked, bent over slightly, shuffling slowly, in those final months.

He can taste the sweetness of those memories.

"Do this in remembrance of me." Luke 22:19

Faux Pas

So here I am, going about my appointed weekend rounds, and I deliver my son to the game arcade where his nine-year-old friend is having his birthday party. I park, get out and walk him to the door of the place. Already, most of the other boys are there, waiting outside for the arcade to open.

I'm thinking about how I have to stop at the store and pick something up and the rest of the seemingly endless list of things I have to do before I return to pick my son up. "I'm going to get going," I tell him. "Give me a kiss."

Even as the words come out of my mouth, I realize the major *faux pas* I've committed.

The other boys look at me as if they're thanking God that I'm no kin of theirs.

My son is looking at his shoes as if he wishes he could shrink down into them.

"My father, the lunkhead," he whispers as he pecks my cheek.

---

*I have become a stranger to my kindred, /an
alien to my mother's children. Psalm 69:8*

September 26

> *Science Fiction Book*

You keep trying to get your son to read that
science fiction book you loved years ago when you
were his age.

Well, actually, you were a little older. He's not
ready for it, and he pretty much ignores you when you
push it on him.

So you have to lay off.

But, boy, you can't wait until he wants to.

---

*The farmer waits for the precious crop from the
earth, being patient with it until it receives the
early and late rains. You also must be patient.
James 5:7-8*

Friends

His kids are great friends to each other. They're two-and-a-half years apart—not so close that they're competitors and not so far apart that they're strangers.

They share funny stories and play games together. They hold entire conversations with a glance.

It's not all that surprising. Their parents are great friends, too.

I take pleasure in three things, /and they are beautiful in the sight of God and of mortals: /agreement among brothers and sisters, friendship among neighbors, /and a wife and a husband who live in harmony. Sirach 25:1

> ## Sleeping Beauty

Her skin is smooth and white as cream. Her eyes are closed, so soft and deep. Her long body is still, except for the movement of her breathing. She is at rest, at peace, asleep.

Her father bends down and tickles the bottom of her foot. Time to get up! Time for another day of first grade! Rise and shine, Sleeping Beauty!

———————————————

Arise, shine; for your light has come, /and the glory of the LORD has risen upon you. Isaiah 60:1

Teachers

You've met your older daughter's teacher. It's going to be a great year! This guy—yes, he's one of the rare men teaching in grade school—is excited to be teaching and enthralled with his subjects. The kids— your daughter and her friends—have caught that excitement, too. She's reading in her spare time, playing math games in the car and drawing maps of everywhere.

You've met the teacher of your younger daughter. This woman is distant, cool, not very interesting.

This daughter's going to have to grit her teeth to make it through the year.

And you're going to have to grit your own teeth while you watch your one girl struggle as the other one soars.

"See. God is exalted in his power; /who is a teacher like him?" Job 36:22

> *Bad Skin*

I ache now about my son's future acne. I cringe at the thought of my daughter's skin marred by pimples.

Bad skin was the horror of my adolescence. I couldn't wait until I was old enough to grow a beard to hide the pock marks.

I want to hug my children now for the pain they will go through when they are teenagers.

Can Ethiopians change their skin /or leopards their spots? /Then also you can do good /who are accustomed to do evil. Jeremiah 13:23

Trading Stories

The first one says his father worked too much.

The second one says his father was weak and never opened his mouth at home.

The third one says his father always ridiculed him.

The fourth one says his father ran away.

The last one says his father loved him.

Faith, hope, and love abide, these three; and the greatest of these is love. 1 Corinthians 13:13

Dialogue

What's your baby's name?

Jennifer.

Why'd you choose that name?

I don't know, Daddy.

How old is she?

One. I mean, zero. She just got born.

Why don't you go over and show Mom.

I did.

What did Mom say?

She's not ready to be a grandmother.

---

*Listen to your father who begot you, /and do
not despise your mother when she is old.
Proverbs 23:22*

Voicemail V

"Hi, Dad. This is your son.

"I'm calling to see—Shut up! I'm leaving a message for Dad!—It's almost my birthday. We're in the yard, playing. Mom's looking at the paper. I'm using the cordless phone. You're upstairs drinking coffee and reading your book. You'll get this message Monday.

"Bye."

Yet you do not even know what tomorrow will bring. What is your life? For you are a mist that appears for a little while and then vanishes. Instead you ought to say, "If the Lord wishes, we will live and do this or that."
James 4:14-15

Evening Scene

He sits on the couch with his wife, listening to a tape of Frank Sinatra.

The lights are low, and he has his arm over her shoulder.

They talk quietly about nothing and everything.

The kids come in every once in a while to ask a question:

"How do you spell . . . ?"

"Can I . . . ?"

"When are we going to . . . ?"

Each time, as they leave, they look back to take it all in.

———————————————

Then we your people, the flock of your pasture, /will give thanks to you forever; /from generation to generation we will recount your praise. Psalm 79:13

Sons and Dads Are Different

For school, my sons writes this:

"Here are some ways that sons and dads are different. For example, dads are old and tall, and sons are young and short. Sons go to school and dads don't. But dads go to work, and sons don't have to. Dads have wedding rings, and sons don't. Sons have toys, and dads aren't supposed to. Dads stay up late, and sons don't. Dads have cars and drive, and sons don't—yet! Dads use the oven, and sons can't."

Let each of you lead the life that the Lord has assigned, to which God called you.
1 Corinthians 7:17

October 6

Lessons

He doesn't cut the grass. He lets the yard service do it. What is he teaching his son?

He's teaching his son that he needs time to take his boy to a movie, or to play catch, or to sit around talking.

He drops his daughter at school early so he can get to the gym to work out before heading into the office. What is he teaching his girl?

He's teaching her that taking care of one's body is good, even if it requires sacrifice and discipline.

He loses his temper and slams doors. What is he teaching his children?

He's teaching them that fathers are imperfect, and that a father can be wrong, and that a father can come back later and say he's sorry.

Make me to know your ways, O LORD; /teach me your paths. Psalm 25:4

> *A Confession*

On Sundays (and Saturdays and Mondays and, on occasion, Thursdays), I like to watch football.

The passes are elegant. The runs are breathtaking. But the hits are what's at the heart of the game.

When a middle-linebacker slams into a willowy receiver just at the moment when the ball arrives—that's football.

I cheer as loud as anyone, maybe louder.

But I hope my son never plays the game.

Does a spring pour forth from the same opening both fresh and brackish water?
James 3:11

It's Unfair: Part I

Forget about the slim, muscular male bodies on the commercials. Guys can still get away with eating a lot and being over-weight.

That thick, juicy steak. That extra large pizza with three kinds of cheese. That big piece of chocolate cake.

Men can eat and eat and eat.

But heaven help the poor woman who puts on some extra pounds.

When people began to multiply on the face of the earth, and daughters were born to them, the sons of God saw that they were fair. Genesis 6:1

It's Unfair: Part II

Your wife is oppressed with options.

Should she work full-time or part-time?

Should she stay home and take care of the kids and the house?

Should she go back to school and get her master's degree?

You wonder what it would be like to have those options.

———————————————

I call aloud, but there is no justice. Job 19:7

Growing Old

Aging, especially in our culture, equals decay.

But growing older can also be a growth process—a process of learning just how much of life I still have to learn.

The older I get, the more I realize I can't know it all . . . and the more I relish those things that I do learn and those people I really do come to know.

In old age they still produce fruit; /they are always green and full of sap. Psalm 92:14

Testimony

The father says: No father gets along completely with his son.

The son says: I love him, but he bugs me. It's as if he goes out of his way to make me angry. He just doesn't understand.

The father says: Sometimes, I ache for that little boy he once was. That boy listened to me. He knew I was his father.

The son says: I don't understand him.

If then I am a father, where is the honor due me? Malachi 1:6

End of the Rainbow

The heavy rain is still pounding down, even as the sun breaks through the clouds.

You stand on the porch and look east and see, up there, a rainbow in all its thin, shimmering beauty.

You go inside and call your son out. He draws rainbows all the time. You want him to see a real one.

But by the time he gets out to the porch, the rain and the clouds and the sun have shifted, and the rainbow is gone.

He goes back inside. You remain, still intoxicated by the wonder you have seen.

There are other rainbows you will share.

I have set my bow in the clouds, and it shall be a sign of the covenant between me and the earth. Genesis 9:13

Dark Heritage

What am I going to do when it comes time to tell my son about rape?

I am shamed by the thought that some men force themselves upon women and turn the act of love into an act of violence. It is a stain on all men, a kind of original sin.

This is a dark part of our heritage as men. I hate it that my son and I share this heritage.

Our ancestors sinned; they are no more, /and we bear their iniquities. Lamentations 5:7

Father of Seven

He loves each of them deeply but not the same.

He holds each one of his seven children close to his heart. But each—an individual—has a slightly different place.

Each is not one of seven but one alone.

He doesn't have seven children. He has Bill and Kevin and Sarah and David and Cathy and Matthias and Robin.

May our sons in their youth /be like plants full grown, /our daughters like corner pillars, /cut for the building of a palace. Psalm 144:12

Dalliances

His daughter is now a young woman, and she looks good—like the women he chased when he was married to her mother.

She won't warm up to him. She keeps him at arm's length. She holds those dalliances against him.

But why should she care? That was between him and her mother.

He's always been her father. He's always loved her.

Even on those nights he stayed away from home.

———————————————

That which is, already has been; that which is to be, already is; and God seeks out what has gone. Ecclesiastes 3:15

Retired

For a year now, my father has had to face the reality of retirement looming on the horizon.

First, his bank was bought by another larger bank, and everyone in the security force—except him—was fired. Talk about survivor guilt.

He was kept as a sort of liaison with the outside firm that would be providing guards. But he had little to do, nothing to keep himself busy. He felt guilty and ashamed to be paid for doing no work.

He was like someone under a death sentence, waiting to be laid off, knowing that it was coming some time, some time. No wonder he told my mother he was blue.

After working week-in and week-out for more than half a century, he couldn't envision a life without the routine—and fulfillment—of work. And, of course, the end of his career is a not-so-subtle reminder that the end of his life isn't too far away.

And now the time has come. He retires in a week. It wasn't his idea.

By faith Abraham obeyed when he was called to set out for a place that he was to receive as an inheritance; and he set out, not knowing where he was going. Hebrews 11:8

And So It Begins

My nine-year-old son brings me the book I left out near my chair.

"Here, Dad," he says.

"Oh. Thank you."

"Dad?"

"Yes."

"What's this book about?"

"It's about what boys go through when they become teenagers. About how your body changes and stuff like that."

"But, Dad, it's got drawings of girls without clothes on."

And so it begins.

Do you not know that your body is a temple of the Holy Spirit within you, which you have from God, and that you are not your own?
1 Corinthians 6:19

Advice

He is astounded by a colleague's deception.

There are no protocols for this. If he were to do something—like bring it to the boss's attention or suggest that the co-worker undo what he has done—he would be treading on forbidden territory.

It is a serious charge to make and back up. And, even if he can back it up, then what?

Still, what would he tell his kids to do in the same situation?

Then King Rehoboam took counsel with the older men who had attended his father Solomon while he was still alive, saying, "How do you advise me to answer this people?" 1 Kings 12:6

> *Jesus Would Agree*

I won't tell my kids that God wants them to keep their rooms clean.

I don't talk to them about sin and vice, or tell them tales of Satan.

I try to talk to them about getting along with others.

I try to teach them to speak their mind, to have opinions, to feel confident, to recognize their goodness.

I try to help them learn how to listen.

I think Jesus would agree.

"'You shall love the Lord your God with all your heart, and with all your soul, and with all your mind.' This is the greatest and first commandment. And a second is like it: 'You shall love your neighbor as yourself.' On these two commandments hang all the law and the prophets." Matthew 22:37-40

Dad's Therapist

He met his father's therapist today, and it was cool.

He'd always known his father saw the therapist once a week on Tuesday mornings. It has been going on for years. But he never really considered what went on there.

Oh, he'd been there once when he was a little guy, but now that he's in college he had asked to come along one day. And his father had agreed.

His dad introduced him to the therapist, and she seemed happy and interested to see him again. She asked about school, and his father bragged about his grades.

His father told him he usually talks abut his feelings in his therapy sessions, and he told the therapist how good it felt to have his son there.

Afterwards, at the train, his Dad hugged him— as he always does—and then went off to work. The son drove to campus in time for his anthropology class. He was whistling.

"Lay aside immaturity, and live, /and walk in the way of insight." Proverbs 9:6

Sequential Parenting

On this warm, fall Sunday, my wife and her friends are in Wisconsin picking apples. I'm here, watching the kids watch their new tape of *Aladdin*.

When she gets home, I'll go out to a movie.

Such are the trade-offs of modern parenthood, particularly when you and your spouse have such different interests.

But it's a complicated balancing act. How much time by herself is enough for my wife? How much time for me? How much for us to be together without the kids? For us to be together with the kids?

And how much individual attention do each of the kids need from each of us? And from the two of us together?

It gets pretty convoluted, although no less important for all the complexity.

Two are better than one, because they have a good reward for their toil. For if they fall, one will lift up the other; but woe to one who is alone and falls and does not have another to help. Ecclesiastes 4:9-10

Not Quite Bitter

He has been overlooked. Again.

The bosses fawn over the hot prospect. They're over-awed by the pompous veteran. They're blinded by their own ideas.

He is ready to chuck it all—if he could live without the salary . . . and the benefits . . . and the joy he gets deep inside when he does his work well.

We do not dare to classify or compare ourselves
with some of those who commend themselves.
But when they measure themselves by one
another, and compare themselves with one
another, they do not show good sense.
2 Corinthians 10:12

Weeds

From his car stalled in traffic, he notices the weeds that hang on tenaciously along a fence as the weather turns cold and the tree leaves turn color and fall.

He knows how tenacious the weeds of his own life are, and what fertile ground they find.

Maybe some of his weeds are wildflowers.

You have been born anew, not of perishable but of imperishable seed, through the living and enduring word of God. For /"All flesh is like grass, /and all its glory like the flower of grass. /The grass withers /and the flower falls, /but the word of the Lord endures forever." 1 Peter 1:23-25

Unemployed

You have no job.

It is as if there is a hole in the world where you stand.

It is as if no one can see you.

The shame is a thick cover over your skin.

You wonder if your kids will think you're a failure.

"He said to them, 'Why are you standing here idle all day?' They said to him, 'Because no one has hired us.'" Matthew 20:6-7

> *Pride*

My son walks down the aisle of my office, dancing with muted movements to the music inside his head. His sister glances from side to side, intensely interested in the doo-dads that my colleagues have on their desks.

We're here to pick up something, just a quick stop. My kids like to see where I work.

When they were younger, they used to like to play here.

They recognize changes in the stuff on and around my desk. They're proud to see their art work on the walls of my cubicle.

My co-workers look up and smile as we walk past.

I'm proud of my children. As they are of me.

"My Father, you are the friend of my youth."
Jeremiah 3:4

Fragile

He is bitter and ready to take offense. "Fragile" is how you'd describe him if such words were used for men.

He's sensitive to any hint that he might not be the perfect worker or the A-1 husband or the All-American father. He's touchy. He has a chip on his shoulder.

It's irritating to hear him whine. But it's also sad to see how unsure he is of himself.

For God did not give us a spirit of cowardice, but rather a spirit of power and of love and of self-discipline. 2 Timothy 1:7

Oh, God

In the car: His teenage daughter, his 10-year-old son and him.

His daughter says: "George likes Sally, doesn't he?"

His son answers: "Yeah, he'd like to kiss her."

Pause.

"I'd like to, too," the boy adds.

Oh, God.

I adjure you, O daughters of Jerusalem, /by the gazelles or the wild does: /do not stir up or awaken love /until it is ready! Song of Songs 2:7

Not the Way

It wasn't supposed to be this way. He was supposed to be the first to go. She would survive him. It was all there in the actuarial tables. It was what they knew would happen. It was what they planned.

But no one told her body that. And when her cells turned traitor, he and she had no time for anything but to hold each other in terror and fierce love.

It's three years now, and he still finds himself making a mental note to tell her of their son's surprising new skill at basketball.

He still looks up from the kitchen table to call to the other room to ask her a question about the mortgage.

He's even started to call home to complain to her about his boss.

This wasn't the way it was supposed to be.

He heals the brokenhearted, /and binds up their wounds. Psalm 147:3

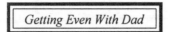

Getting Even With Dad

You are hiking with your son, and you are out of breath. He is several turns ahead of you on the trail.

This is the state park where, years ago, you and the rest of the family had to slow down and keep stopping so this same boy could catch up. It's where your son kept tripping on the tree roots he hadn't learned yet to look for on the trail.

And now, when he's a teenager, it's where he's outdistancing his father and is halfway up the slope.

I have taught you the way of wisdom, /I have led you in the paths of uprightness. /When you walk, your step will not be hampered; /and if you run, you will not stumble. Proverbs 4:11-12

| Anniversary |

You are the fire of my life.

You burn with truth.

You flame with life.

You light my way.

Through all our joys,

Through all our conflicts,

Through all the routine of our days,

I love you.

Eat, friends, drink, /and be drunk with love.
Song of Songs 5:1

Easy as Pie

Here, children, is a story for you:

There was a young man (well, not so young, 31) who called up a newly met friend, a woman of 26.

She had a broken leg, and he suggested they go for a ride to look at the fall colors.

They did and fell in love.

It was easy as pie.

"It is not good that man should be alone."
Genesis 2:18

> *Dear Boss*

Welcome to parenthood!

If you're as lucky as my wife and I have been, you and your husband will find it the most fun, enriching, enlivening, entertaining (and, yes, on rare occasion, aggravating) experience of your lives.

Much happy congratulations on your daughter's birth!

_____

Sing praises to the Lord, for he has done gloriously; /let this be known in all the earth.
Isaiah 12:5

The Meaning of Fatherhood: Part 6

Your daughter vomits on the living room floor.

You put your arm gently on her shoulder and lead her to the bathroom.

You crouch next to her and watch as she vomits again and again and again.

You say soft words. You wipe her forehead. You give her water.

She's breathing easier now, although she's still pale. You give her some stomach medicine and carry her to bed.

You say more soft words. You pat her arms. You smooth her hair.

Then, as she drops off the sleep, finally at peace, you go out to the living room to clean up the floor.

The fruit of the Spirit is love, joy, peace, patience, kindness, generosity, faithfulness, gentleness, and self-control. Galatians 5:22-23

How to Care for Babies

There once was a father from Winston

Whose smile on his babies did glisten.

He hoisted them, hugged them,

Changed them and lugged them,

And, whenever he could, he did kiss them.

Steadfast love and faithfulness will meet;
/righteousness and peace will kiss each other.
Psalm 85:10

Odd Couple

He's so big, and his father's so small. He's young and tall and muscular and tanned. His father is, well, old and short and skinny and pale.

He lifts weights, swims and runs. His father pushes a pencil.

It's been this way since early high school when he shot up in a growth spurt that took him well past his father.

The Old Man smiles a crooked grin, half embarrassed to be so puny.

But oh-so-proud of his giant of a son.

The least of them shall become a clan, /and the smallest one a mighty nation. Isaiah 60:22

Phenom

He's a phenom. He's always ready to swing for the fences. His co-workers look at him with awe. He knows this. He thinks this is his due. He is young. He is skilled. He is intoxicated by the success that comes his way, as it should. He works late. He works weekends. He's moving up. He's on the rise. He's bursting with ideas, exploding with energy. He tells his wife it's only until he's established. He has to make his mark. On the way out in the morning, he kisses his baby daughter on the forehead as she sleeps. When he comes in at night, he tip-toes into her room to kiss her again. He doesn't wake her.

Again, I saw vanity under the sun; the case of solitary individuals, without sons or brothers; yet there is no end to all their toil, and their eyes are never satisfied with riches.
Ecclesiastes 4:7-8

Fairness

I'm putting my daughter to bed, and she's telling about first grade and her frustrations.

"It's not fair," she says.

The fifth-graders came in today to help the first-graders write Thanksgiving stories. My daughter was hoping that one particular fifth-grader would help her, but, instead, the girl went as usual to help the one she always helps.

"It's not fair," my daughter says.

This is a frequent refrain from her, and I try to explain that life often isn't fair.

"Well, isn't it good to be fair?"

"Yes, but. . . ."

"Then, life should be fair."

I can't argue with that.

"Will not God grant justice to his chosen ones who cry to him day and night? Will he delay long in helping them? I tell you, he will quickly grant justice to them." Luke 18:7-8

Election Day

They go together to the polling place at the local police station.

It is morning, early. The father is on his way to work. The kids he'll drop at the babysitter's when he's done.

As he stands over the rickety voting stand with its punch-card ballot, he explains to his five-year-old daughter what he's doing. She seems more impressed by the poster of a cartoon bad guy on the police station wall. His infant son sucks on the pacifier as the father holds him in his left arm and votes with his right hand.

He moves quickly through the ballot. Some offices he skips. He knows nothing of either candidate.

On the way out, he explains to the children that voting is like church—sacred, even if it's sometimes a bit of a duty.

His daughter examines another poster.

———————————

Let us choose what is right; /let us determine among ourselves what is good. Job 34:4

Belly-button Laughter

We giggle in the kitchen.

My son is cleaning out his belly-button with such intense interest that he draws everyone's attention. My wife and I can't stop laughing.

His sister gets in the act, transforming her belly-button into the snout of a pig.

We all laugh.

And laugh.

And laugh.

Belly-button laughter.

"God has brought laughter for me; everyone who hears will laugh with me." Genesis 21:6

November 9

One A.M.

It's one A.M., and he's two hours late. You're sitting
up, unable to read, wondering, worrying, angry, afraid,
unable to pay attention to the colorful empty surfaces
of the shows on the TV, drinking another beer, eating
some more nacho chips, remembering how he was—
so bright and filled with life—when he went to
kindergarten that first day, remembering how he
yelled at you a week ago over his chores and you
yelled back, remembering the small round scar at his
left temple from the long-ago case of chicken pox,
worrying, wondering, angry and afraid.

_"For the promise is for you, for your children,
and for all who are far away, everyone whom
the Lord our God calls to him." Acts 2:39_

A Breakfast Conference

My six-year-old daughter says to her nine-year-old brother: "I'm going to Taylor's house after school. So when Beth picks you up, you won't have to wait for me."

He nods.

"Except Taylor might be sick. So come over an look for me before you go."

He nods.

"Okay?"

"Okay," he says, and goes back to his Cheerios.

They're got it all arranged. And I've got one more thing to worry about today.

When the cares of my heart are many, /your consolations cheer my soul. Psalm 94:19

November 11

The Argument

The argument took an hour to run its course.

It started in the kitchen, moved to the front room, and they finally thrashed it out in their bedroom, sitting at first at opposite ends of the bed but ending up next to each other, consoling each other.

When they came out, the children were on the hallway floor in front of their door, putting puzzles together.

Be angry but do not sin; do not let the sun go down on your anger, and do not make room for the devil. Ephesians 4:26

In the Checkout Line

The boy, just six, looks up at his father as they stand together in the checkout line at the grocery.

The man he sees towers over him, filled with power. He has money and muscles and a knowledge of the way things work.

The man is scary, especially when he's angry. But he still cradles the boy in his strong arms. His shoulder is a soft place where the boy likes to rest his head.

The man can drive a car. He can pick up a desk. He knows about kissing and going to work and how to fix a car.

The boy understands that, someday, he will stand in a line like this with his own son. But he can't imagine how.

———————————

*"Be strong, be courageous, and keep the charge of the L*ORD *your God, walking in his ways."*
1 Kings 2:2

Third Father

The boy is on his third father.

This one is nice enough if you don't mind the grease in his hair and the unfiltered Camels he smokes. He's not bad.

He took the boy to Sears for the bike he asked for. He explained how a carburetor works in a way the boy could understand. He doesn't do any hitting.

But he's only a substitute father.

His real father is long gone.

Have we not all one father? Has not one God created us? Why then are we faithless to one another? Malachi 2:10

Who's Embarrassed?

He's afraid of what his father will think of his fiance's parents. They're simple people. Her dad runs a convenience store. Her mom works in a school cafeteria. They don't have a lot of education. They don't always use correct grammar.

He's afraid his father will make fun of them— the way he makes fun of everyone.

He's afraid his father will tease her parents and make the woman he's going to marry feel embarrassed over them.

She's not the one who should be embarrassed.

———————————————

"All who exalt themselves will be humbled, and all who humble themselves will be exalted."
Matthew 23:12

| The Last Time |

Which will be the very last time I pick my son up in my arms?

He's getting so big and doing so much on his own.

But, for now, he still likes—but only every once in a while—to have me pick him up. Usually, it's to carry him to bed.

I love doing it, but I know it can't last forever.

A time to embrace, and a time to refrain from embracing. Ecclesiastes 3:5

Late Fall

Winter is nearly here. I can hardly wait. The snow will turn the city into a thing of beauty. It will crunch beneath my feet. It will float down with infinite gentleness to touch my face, my eyebrows.

I know winter can be cruel. It will make my kids sick. It will cause my car to die. It will be a frigid hell for those who have no home and can't find warmth.

I know all that.

But, still, I'm waiting for the beauty of the snow.

The eye is dazzled by the beauty of its white-ness, /and the mind is amazed as it falls.
Sirach 43:18

> ### A Question and Three Answers

Question: What happens when you die? What happens to all you have learned, all your wisdom? What happens to all the love you've given, all the love you've received?

Answer #1: It all disappears.

Answer #2: You go to heaven and everything becomes somehow even richer—the wisdom, wiser; the love, deeper.

Answer #3: There's no way to know.

"Everyone who drinks of this water will be thirsty again, but those who drink of the water that I will give them will never be thirsty. The water that I will give will become in them a spring of water gushing up to eternal life."
John 4:13-14

Good Lives

Your co-worker's father, frail and ailing, dies suddenly on the holiday. You offer condolences.

That same day, your son in third grade writes a long meandering story about a boy. It starts when the hero is a baby and ends when he is 89-years-old.

"Then he died," your son writes. "It was a good life."

Yes, it was.

The glory of youths is their strength, /but the beauty of the aged is their gray hair. Proverbs 20:29

Good Eating

My six-year-old daughter brings home her own recipe for cooking a turkey:

Wash it in the sink.

Chop off the head.

Stuff it with cake.

Cook it at six degrees for one minute.

"Have you never read, /'Out of the mouths of infants and nursing babies /you have prepared praise for yourself'?" Matthew 21:16

Thank You, God

On the Wednesday before Thanksgiving, my son brings home this prayer of his own composition:

"Thank you, God, for the animals that you made—for the owls that hoot, for the tigers that roar, for the fish that swim, for the parrots that fly, and for all the animals in the world.

"Thank you, God, for the beautiful gardens—for the pretty flowers that smell so sweet, for the plants so green, for the trees so tall, for the shade from the trees, and for all the gardens on earth.

"Thank you, God, for autumn so beautiful—for the pumpkins on Halloween, for the leaves that fall, for the Thanksgiving dinners, for the joy of autumn and for all these wonderful things.

"Thank you, God, for our family—for our brothers and sisters, for our moms and dads, for our grandmas and grandpas, for our cousins, and for all the people and their families.

"Thank you, God, for friends—for friends when you are sick, for friends to talk to and have fun with, for friends that love you, and for best friends to share special moments with."

Who can utter the mighty doings of the LORD, /or declare all his praise? Psalm 105:2

Thanksgiving

For the cold crisp air of morning.

For the sound of a laughing child.

For the apple's crunch.

For the smell of fresh mown grass.

For awe and wonder and mystery.

Let us thank God.

Let us come into his presence with thanksgiving; /let us make a joyful noise to him with songs of praise! Psalm 95:2

Birthday

I remember how proud I used to be on my birthday. I was another year older. That meant I was another year smarter, another year stronger.

I was me.

Now, I am him—this old guy getting older, getting weaker, no longer able to run the basketball floor with as much speed or as much spirit.

I know more. But I know how much I don't know.

And I'm afraid that all the wisdom that I have so painfully and painstakingly acquired will disappear, evaporate the moment I die.

My child, from your youth choose discipline, /and when you have gray hair you will still find wisdom. Sirach 6:18

A Baby Cries

He hears a baby cry outside in the dark, and he remembers.

His boy, when he was a baby, cried all the time. He would rock his son, and it didn't help. He would hold the boy on his shoulder. He would cradle him in his arms. He would sing to him. Nothing worked. The boy still cried.

His girl didn't cry so much.

It's been years since he's seen either one. The boy was doing odd jobs in Georgia, the last he heard. The girl wouldn't say what she was doing.

Outside, in the dark, a baby cries.

_____

I will say to the north, "Give them up," /and to the south, "Do not withhold; /bring my sons from far away /and my daughters from the end of the earth." Isaiah 43:6

> Getting Older

I find, for the first time in my life, that I don't want my bosses to know my age.

When I look into a lifetime membership at the museum, I go through some complicated computations to figure out if one lump sum payment would be cheaper than simply paying the annual membership dues. (It would be, but not by much.)

I look at aged fathers with grown sons and start to see myself.

I have been young, and now am old. Psalm 37:25

$$\boxed{Gone}$$

So where is that man who gave you life and then walked away when you were twelve?

You are angry with him for leaving. But you also want to pour down on him all the love you had for him then and have had for him ever since.

He should have been there when you needed him. He should have been there to hear you say, "I love you."

Instead, he left.

"And forgive us our debts, /as we also have forgiven our debtors." Matthew 6:12

Working at Home

I am trying to work.

My daughter comes up, smiling, to show me the costume she has fashioned from a pair of sunglasses, a red scarf and a baby blanket.

I am trying to work.

She comes to sing me a song. Her eyes blaze as she tries to remember the words.

I am trying to work.

She tells me her number one favorite teacher. And her number two favorite teacher. And her number three favorite teacher. And her number four favorite teacher. And she's only in first grade.

I am trying to work.

She shows me her number one favorite doll. And her number two favorite doll. And. . . .

When Moses saw that they had done all the work just as the LORD had commanded, he blessed them. Exodus 39:43

> *Not the Foggiest*

We are watching Walt Disney's *Fantasia*, and it is at the point in the movie's interpretation of Stravinsky's *Firebird* when the dinosaurs are searching vainly for water, and dying.

"Why isn't there any water, Dad?" my daughter asks.

"Because it hasn't rained."

"Why hasn't it rained?"

"I don't know. I guess the weather changed."

Pause.

"Dad, why is God letting the dinosaurs die? He's the one making it not rain. Why is he making them die?"

Should I answer with an explanation of free will, and a world moving along within the rules of nature, and the randomness of life, and the constancy of change, and the fickleness of luck?

Nah. I admit I don't have the foggiest idea.

"Has the rain a father, /or who has begotten the drops of dew?" Job 38:28

The Meeting

You go to your parents' house. You sit down with them and your sister. You listen as they go through one file folder after another, explaining their pensions, their investments, their insurance policies and their wills. It has come to this: They are getting their lives in order.

There is an element of play-acting to this. You cannot imagine them dead. Neither can they, not really.

But the time is coming.

So teach us to count our days /that we may gain a wise heart. Psalms 90:12

Delivery Truck

It was a good job when he was young. Tiring, of course. But he'd bounce back every morning, and his muscles grew stronger.

Now, the cases are heavier. His back is stiffer. His feet hurt. His legs ache. He doesn't jump out of the truck's cab anymore. He climbs slowly down and moves along the truck one step at a time and takes a deep breath before opening the door and starting to unload.

He pictures his son at a computer terminal in a downtown office building and envies him.

Do not cast me off in the time of old age; /do not forsake me when my strength is spent. Psalm 71:9

A Day Off

I got the kids up, fed them and got them over to school.   And tonight, I'll take them to a skating party.

But until then, I'm free. It's my day off, and I'm sitting in the quiet, drinking coffee and reading a novel. In an hour or so, I'll go get a haircut and maybe see a movie.

My wife is at work, and it's as if I was single again.

I'm deep in my novel. The hero is on a Mediterranean island, sparring with a beautiful female spy. His wife and children are hundreds of miles away in England.

Now write what you have seen, what is, and what is to take place after this. Revelation 1:19

December 1

| Gotcha |

I'm home alone with my nine-year-old son. I'm doing the crossword puzzle, and he's talking to me.

"Dad, do you know how fast a cheetah can run?"

"Dad, why is this called a Mercury dime?"

"Dad, what's this other puzzle on the page?"

"Dad, how do they make dollar bills?"

"Dad, how do they stop people in banks from stealing the money?"

Each time, I look up and try to answer.

"Dad, does it bother you sometimes when I ask a lot of questions? Like now?"

He's got me there.

"I will question you, and you declare to me."
Job 42:4

The Fragility of Love

He and his wife grieved at their inability to conceive a child.

The effort strained their marriage. There were so many tests, so many records to keep, so many schedules to meet, so much to worry about.

It broke their love.

Now, he walks a dog alone in the cool breeze of a spring evening.

If two lie together, they keep each other warm;
but how can one keep warm alone?
Ecclesiastes 4:11

Playtime

Tonight, my kids played jewel thief. My nine-year-old son put his gray suit on and a tie over his white t-shirt. He had no socks or shoes on.

My six-year-old daughter carried two briefcases and listened skeptically to the jewel thief's smooth talk.

Then, my daughter was a dentist, checking out the teeth of a woman and her baby son. The woman was my wife. The baby was my son, the former jewel thief.

I worked throughout it all, listening with half an ear to their play... and wishing I could join them.

The streets of the city shall be full of boys and girls playing. Zechariah 8:5

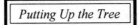

Putting Up the Tree

Early on, my wife and I came up with a division of labor for putting up the Christmas tree.

I haul the (fake) tree up from the basement (in two boxes), set up the stand and go through the painstaking but mindless process of putting the (metal and plastic) branches into the (two-piece, detachable) trunk of the tree.

This is what my father did each Christmas, keeping all of us kids—14 eventually—away from him through a combination of mutterings, grumblings and glares.

I took the same attitude at first, but, maybe because I have only two kids or maybe because I'm a different person, I grew to enjoy having my children hanging around watching while I went about the monotonous task.

And, as they grew older, they were able to begin to help until, this year, they carried out easily half of the job.

Another year or two and I'll be the one watching.

My wife? Her job is to decorate the tree. I know my limits.

They are like trees /planted by streams of water, /which yield their fruit in its season, /and their leaves do not wither. Psalm 1:3

Limits

Testing.

My son orders me to find his glove.

Testing.

My daughter demands her lunch—now!

Testing.

The children won't put on their seatbelts.

Testing.

They turn on the TV that I've just turned off.

They're testing their limits.

They're also testing my patience.

---

*He must manage his own household well,
keeping his children submissive and respectful
in every way—for if someone does not know
how to manage his own household, how can he
take care of God's church? 1 Timothy 3:4-5*

Emotions

You see the morning sunrise on your way to work and have no words for the wonder.

You feel the stab of fear at your daughter's sudden scream in the night.

The exact, intricate movements of a squirrel—eating a scrap of bread, skittering across the grass, scaling a tree—fascinate you.

You are vaguely sad to see the house down the street torn down.

The grocery bag breaks in your hands, and you are startled.

———————————————

A new heart I will give you, and a new spirit I will put within you; and I will remove from your body the heart of stone and give you a heart of flesh. Ezekiel 36:26

First Snow

In the lingering dark before dawn, a loud yell explodes into the air.

"Yaaaaaaaahoo! It snowed last night!!!"

My son, normally slow to stir on school mornings, is not only out of bed but in the living room, dancing, jumping, bounding with delight.

He shouts to his sister, "Look! It snowed last night!"

He sends out his command to the earth; /his word runs swiftly. /He gives snow like wool; /he scatters frost like ashes. Psalm 147:15-16

Skipping

Coming home from the babysitter's house, the children skip.

Remember the last time you skipped?

Don't you wish you could skip now?

Wouldn't look right. You're wearing your business suit now. You're an adult. A man of the world.

Aw, go ahead and skip.

Let them praise his name with dancing, /making melody to him with tambourine and lyre.
Psalm 149:3

Recognition

I'm a good father. I love my kids. I listen to them. I talk to them.

We share our lives together.

This is good for me to recognize.

I bow my knees before the Father, from whom every family in heaven and on earth takes its name. Ephesians 3:14-15

The Compound Machine

My son is dancing through the house. He and my wife have just finished putting together the "compound machine" that has been his special homework assignment for the past two weeks.

It was his own idea and design: an inclined plane and a can at the end of a pulley—hence, a "compound machine."

It is, he writes in his cover explanation, patterned after a downtown parking lot—sort of. You put a toy car on the inclined plane (the first machine—a triangular piece of wood from an old set of blocks), and it rolls to the edge where it falls, nose first, into the can. Then you turn the pulley (the second machine—made with string and a pencil and a couple twisted paper clips) to raise the car back up.

His mother is drained after working three nights in a row with him on the project.

I am just a proud bystander.

We are God's servants, working together; you are God's field, God's building. 1 Corinthians 3:9

December 11

Jobs

You work two jobs, and a third one when you've got the time.

It's all you can do to keep food on the table and clothes on your children.

You don't have any special skills. But you're willing to work. You do your best. You try.

Your children ask: "Dad, when are you coming home?"

We appeal to you, brothers and sisters, to respect those who labor among you, and have charge of you in the Lord and admonish you; esteem them very highly in love because of their work. 1 Thessalonians 5:12-13

Nativity Scenes

The kids are excited.

They put up the crib scene—Mary, Joseph, Baby Jesus and assorted hangers-on that my son made in first grade—atop the air conditioner in the front window.

They put the one he made in second grade on my daughter's dresser.

The creche that my wife and I received on our first Christmas as a married couple they put in a window in the dining room.

And, on the hutch, they put a later acquisition—a collection of wooden figures, carved in a simple manner—and flank this with two electric candles.

They're like little doll houses, all these ramshackle Nativity scenes.

And little sacraments, as well.

He is the image of the invisible God, the firstborn of all creation; for in him all things in heaven and on earth were created. Colossians 1:15-16

What He Has

He has a daughter, by his first wife, working in Sacramento. He has a son, by his second wife, still in high school in Milwaukee.

And here he is married again, and a father again.

The little boy has just turned three, and his eyes dart around the room with a fierce gusto for life.

His father watches and tries to remember if the other ones were as intense.

Or as rewarding.

The wise have eyes in their head, /but fools walk in darkness. Ecclesiastes 2:14

Words

He is, as usual, at a loss for words.

His wife is raging. His kids are crying. The pipe in the bathroom has broken—again. And the mortgage is three weeks overdue.

In his head, amid the swirl, all he can hear is one work: "Caught."

He would like to sing a song at the top of his lungs. But he doesn't know the words.

———————————

It is an unhappy business that God has given to human beings to be busy with. Ecclesiastes 1:13

December 15

You tell your children to be honest. But you also make sure they don't tell Aunt Ellen that she has bad breath.

You tell your children to be observant. But you also make sure they know not to point at the oddly dressed man on the bus.

You hope they learn the subtler lessons as well, such as:

(1) Get a job. But not one that will take over your life.

(2) Keep a neat house. But don't be so fussy that you drive people away.

(3) Be responsible. But have fun, too.

She makes linen garments and sells them; /she supplies the merchant with sashes. /Strength and dignity are her clothing, /and she laughs at the time to come. Proverbs 31:24-25

| Burned |

My son burns his finger on his mother's curling iron. Ouch! Do we put ice or butter on it?

He's mad that we didn't protect him from the pain, and we feel guilty. After all, it's our job to keep him safe.

But we can't keep him safe from everything.

That's not much of a consolation—to him or to us.

I led them with cords of human kindness, /with bands of love. /I was to them like those /who lift infants to their cheeks. /I bent down to them and fed them. Hosea 11:4

So Young

He's so young. Too young to be a father. But there he is, holding his baby daughter in his arms. Smiling that befuddled grin that all fathers have. But his befuddlement is deeper. His amazement, too. His confusion. His fear. He is so young. And so is his baby.

Shun youthful passions and pursue righteousness, faith, love, and peace, along with those who call on the Lord from a pure heart.
2 Timothy 2:22

Too Much Fun

My work is much too much fun. I have what everyone desires—an interesting job. So I have to be careful. If I'm not strict with myself, I end up working too many extra hours.

As it is, I throw myself so totally into my work that often I'm drained when I get home, no good for anyone.

And then there are all the extra things—the free-lance jobs, the church committees, the exercise class.

I am pulled away from my wife and kids. It's too tempting.

"You say, 'I am rich, I have prospered, and I need nothing,' You do not realize that you are wretched, pitiable, poor, blind, and naked."
Revelation 3:17

December 19

It's a Wonderful Life

Near the end of *It's a Wonderful Life*, the angel Clarence has come down from heaven and is showing George Bailey (Jimmy Stewart) what life in Bedford Falls would have been like if he had never been born.

You watch, and you start to day-dream. You look at your children and try to picture a world without them. If you hadn't been born, they wouldn't exist. No one would have seen their smiles. No one would have dried their tears. No one would have hugged them—or been hugged back.

They are so alive. They are so real.

They had to exist. From the beginning of time, they had to be born and live their lives. Anything else would be absurd. Anything else would be unthinkable.

It's a wonderful life.

You brought them in and planted them on the mountain of your own possession, /the place, O Lord, that you made your abode, /the sanctuary, O Lord, that your hands have established.
Exodus 15:17

Lonely

Lonely is when I'm on a business trip. Lonely is when I'm mad at everybody at home, and they know I've gone over the line. Lonely is the way it was before I met my wife, before we had our children. Lonely is when my son is in a hurry to run out to play with his friend down the block. Lonely is when my daughter walks by herself to the school door, her back-pack slung casually over her shoulder, her head held high. Lonely is all those unshareable joys, those unutterable fears, those inarticulate longings. Lonely is knowing that an end will come, and I'll face it alone.

Do your best to come to me soon, for Demas, in love with this present world, has deserted me and gone to Thessalonica; Crescens has gone to Galatia, Titus to Dalmatia. Only Luke is with me. 2 Timothy 4:9-11

Prepared

One morning, when he was seven, he was awakened and told his grandfather was dead.

When he was 25, he stood with his sister at his grandmother's bedside. The next day, she was dead.

Now he is middle-aged. His parents are frail.

He is not ready.

Neither are his children.

"In my Father's house there are many dwelling places. If it were not so, would I have told you that I go to prepare a place for you? And if I go and prepare a place for you, I will come again and will take you to myself, so that where I am, there you may be also." John 14:2-3

Blame

The children blame themselves. But it wasn't their fault.

You want to blame her. She's the one who walked out. But it's not so simple. You know that.

Deep down, you know how you added to the pain that broke up your marriage.

But it's too painful to think of that now—now when you're filled with so much anger and hurt.

You want to hug the children to take away their fear. You want them to hug you to take away your loneliness.

They look at you out of the corner of their eyes.

As it is said, /"Today, if you hear his voice,
/do not harden your hearts as in the rebellion."
Hebrews 3:15

Stories

My son wants to hear stories of when I was a child. I can remember only a few.

I ask my father about his childhood. He doesn't remember much either.

In my desk at home, I keep file folders for each year for each of the children. They are stuffed with drawings, homework assignments, letters, awards. And I've always got my camera out, taking pictures of them.

If my children can't remember their stories when they're grown, these things may help them make some up.

"I thank you, Father, Lord of heaven and earth, because you have hidden these things from the wise and the intelligent and have revealed them to the childlike; yes, Father, for such was your gracious will." Matthew 11:25-26

| '*Twas the Night before Christmas* |

He is tired. It has been a long day.

His wife is tired. She's overdue and uncomfortable and preoccupied. She's patiently waiting for him to find them a place to stay.

They should never have taken this trip so close to her due date. But there you have it. They did, and here he is, scrambling around in the night, trying to find a bed in a city crowded with visitors.

She is sitting awkwardly when he gets back, her legs apart, her belly huge. She smiles weakly to him.

He leans down and gives her a kiss. Then he sits down next to her.

They are sitting silently together when the pains of birth begin.

While they were there, the time came for her to deliver her child. And she gave birth to her first-born son and wrapped him in bands of cloth, and laid him in a manger, because there was no place for them in the inn. Luke 2:6-7

Unmerry Christmas

How could my son be sick?

He was three, and this was his first Christmas really knowing what the holiday was all about—at least the Santa part of the holiday. He'd been so excited.

So why was it, when the day finally came, that all he wanted to do was sleep? Why did he have such a deep fever? Why was he so weighed down with his illness that he had no desire at all to rouse himself for the celebration?

And why, except for watching over him, was there nothing I could do?

"Do not fear, only believe." Mark 5:36

Not as Crazy?

You look around at the chaos of the day after Christmas, and you realize that things aren't as crazy as they used to be.

Your daughter is in her room, moving furniture and dolls around her new dollhouse. Your son is walking back and forth with a set of earphones on his head and a small radio in his hand.

They're not babies any more. They have their own opinions. They're sure about their likes and dislikes.

Sometimes, it's like living with two teenagers.

Oh, boy.

Brothers and sisters, do not be children in your thinking; rather, be infants in evil, but in thinking be adults. 1 Corinthians 14:20

$$\boxed{\textit{Voicemail VI}}$$

"Hi, Dad. This is your daughter.

"If you're not there right now—what's today? Monday? Wednesday?—it's Tuesday, Dad.

"I don't know if you're there. I'm feeling great. I love you.

"Bye."

To those who are called, who are beloved in God the father and kept safe for Jesus Christ: May mercy, peace, and love be yours in abundance. Jude 1

The Promised Land

Gone are the diapers; college is far in the future.

I play a game of checkers with my daughter before she goes to bed.

I look in on my son as he reads before falling asleep.

My wife looks up from her knitting and smiles.

This is the land of milk and honey.

The LORD brought us out of Egypt with a mighty hand and an outstretched arm, with a terrifying display of power, and with signs and wonders; and he brought us into this place and gave us this land, a land flowing with milk and honey.
Deuteronomy 26:8-9

Gregory

He was the one poor boy in your grade school class. He dressed in wrinkled, dirty clothes. He fell asleep in class. He smelled. He talked funny.

You weren't his friend. No one was. But he'd talk to you. And you'd talk to him.

In a gesture you still don't understand, you took his name for confirmation.

Where is Gregory now?

———————————————

"Do not be afraid, my son, because we have become poor. You have great wealth if you fear God and flee from every sin and do what is good in the sight of the Lord your God." Tobit 4:21

Tantrums

His daughter gets mad and throws a ball of paper across the room.

His wife gets mad and slams down the telephone.

He gets mad and bellows like a bull.

So much rage, so much pain.

Refrain from anger, and forsake wrath. /Do not fret—it leads only to evil. Psalm 37:8

> New Year's Eve

The children are asleep. My wife is at a party. I'm home alone, ready for bed at 10:30. I never was much for parties.

The house is dark except for the light in the living room.

The quiet is like a prayer, an inarticulate sigh.

Another day. Another year. Another ending.

He alone is my rock and my salvation, /my fortress; I shall not be shaken. /On God rests my deliverance and my honor; /my mighty rock, my refuge is in God. Psalm 62:6-7